# A-Z VISITORS' LONDON
## ATLAS and GUIDE

## CONTENTS

G............
Fairfield P................................................PP

Show....

D0596860

An A-Z Pub................................................n 26

Note 1. Each place name is followed by the reference to its map position; e.g. **Admiralty** Whitehall is to be found in square 4A on page 82.

(Places preceded by an *asterisk are outside Central London area mapped.)

Note 2. Each station name is followed by the reference/s (abbreviated) to the Underground Line/s (or outside the Underground network the Main Line Railway Station) serving it. For example, Goodge Street N. means that station is on the Underground Northern Line.

Abbreviations are: B=Bakerloo; Cen.=Central; Cir.=Circle; D.=District; H.=Hammersmith & City; J.=Jubilee; M.=Metropolitan; N.=Northern; P.=Piccadilly; V. =Victoria.

*For central area Underground Map, see back cover.*

## RECOMMENDED SIGHTSEEING

✪✪✪ Places not to be missed
✪✪ Highly recommended
✪ Recommended
✪ Recommended for families with children

■ **Admiralty,** Whitehall. 4A 82
Once the administrative and operational centre of the British Navy, it has become the headquarters of the Home Civil Service. The old building dates from 1722, the handsome screen by Adam being added in 1760. There are valuable paintings and furniture in Admiralty House.
*Station:* Charing Cross B.N.

■ **Admiralty Arch,** Trafalgar Square. 3A 82  ✪
This large triple archway opens on to the Mall and the quiet of St. James's Park. State and Royal processions pass through it on their way between Buckingham Palace and Westminster Abbey and/or the Houses of Parliament.
*Station:* Charing Cross B.N.

■ **Albert Memorial,** Kensington Gardens. 1E 89  ✪
Designed by Sir Gilbert Scott, it was erected as a memorial to Prince Albert, Consort of Queen Victoria, at a cost of £120,000, and took 20 years to construct.
*Station:* South Kensington Cir.D.P.

■ **Alexander Fleming Museum,** St Mary's Hospital, Praed

Street. 4A 66    The laboratory in which Fleming discovered penicillin, displays and video presentation. Open: 10 a.m. to 1 p.m. Mon. to Thurs. and other times by appointment.    *Station:* Paddington B.Cir.D.H

■ **Apsley House,** Hyde Park Corner. 5A 80    ✪
This Adam's building was bought by the famous Duke of Wellington as his London House. It is now the Wellington Museum and contains trophies of the Napoleonic Wars, uniforms, swords and decorations.
*Admission Charge.* Open: Tues to Sun. 11 a.m. to 5 p.m.; Closed: Mon., Christmas Eve and Day and Boxing D. *Station:* Hyde Park Corner P.

■ **Bank of England,** Threadneedle Street. 5F 73
Known as the 'Old Lady of Threadneedle Street' this is the Governments Bank, incorporated under Royal Charter in 1694 to find for the Government £1,200,000 required for the war against France's Louis XIV. Only the massive external wall survives of Sir John Soanes' design of 1833. *Station:* Bank Cen.N.

■ **Bank of England Museum,** Bartholomew Lane. 4F 73
The history of the Bank of England from its foundation in 1694 to its role today as the nation's central bank. Displays include banknotes, coins, gold bullion, interactive videos and a reconstructed 18th century banking hall.
Open: Mon. to Fri. 10 a.m. to 5 p.m. Closed Sat. and Sun. *Station:* Bank Cen.N.

■ **Bankside Gallery,** Hopton Street. 2C 84
Gallery of the Royal Society of Painters in Water-Colours and Royal Society of Painter-Etchers and Engravers.
Open during exhibitions 10 a.m. to 8 p.m. Tues. 10 a.m. to 5 p.m. Wed. to Fri. 1 p.m. to 5 p.m. Sunday. Closed Monday. *Station:* Blackfriars.Cir.D. Southwark. J.

■ **Banqueting House,** Whitehall 4B 82    ✪✪
Commissioned by James I, and built by Inigo Jones it was completed in 1622; and embellished by Charles I, with the famous painted ceiling by Rubens. The artist was rewarded with £3,000 and a knighthood. It was through a window of the Banqueting House that King Charles went to his execution in 1649. It is the only surviving building of Whitehall Palace.    *Admission Charge.* Open: 10 a.m. to 5 p.m. Closed: Sun. *Stations:* Charing Cross B.N., Westminster Cir.D.J.

■ **Barbican.** 2E 73    ✪
A large area of post-war redevelopment designed to reintroduce a balanced residential and cultural life back into the heart of the business City. Pedestrians are segregated from traffic on elevated levels, and accommodation is grouped around squares, gardens and

lakes. The historic church of St. Giles and a length of the Roman and Medieval City Wall are incorporated. The precinct includes the following: Barbican Centre for Arts and Conferences, Museum of London, Guildhall School of Music and Drama, City of London School for Girls. Opened in 1982 the Barbican Arts Centre is the London equivalent of the Lincoln Center, New York or the Centre Pompidou, Paris; facilities include: Barbican Hall, Barbican Theatre, The Pit (studio theatre), Barbican Library, Art Gallery, Cinemas, conference and trade exhibition space, roof-top Conservatory, restaurants and car park.

*Stations:* Barbican Cir.M.H., Moorgate Cir.M.H.

■ **Battle of Britain Museum.** See Outer London. ✪ ✪

■ **BBC Experience,** Broadcasting House, Portland Place. 3C 68 ✪ ✪ Explore the BBC, past, present and future through audio visual shows and interactive displays which take visitors on a guided tour of its history and programmes. Broadcasting House is itself a famous landmark in art deco style, completed in 1932.

*Admission Charge.* Open 9am to 5pm daily, by timed ticket only (pre bookings Tel: 0870 6030304).

*Station:* Oxford Circus B.Cen.V.

■ **Belfast H.M.S.,** Morgan's Lane. 3C 86 ✪ ✪ This 10,500 ton cruiser, launched in 1938, the last major warship of the 1939-45 war still afloat, is now a naval museum. A ferry service runs from Tower Pier.

*Admission Charge.* Open: Summer 10 a.m. to 6 p.m., Winter 10 a.m. to 5 p.m. Closed Christmas Eve and Day Boxing Day, New Year.

*Station:* London Bridge J.N.

■ **\*Bethnal Green Museum of Childhood,** Cambridge Heath Road, E2. ✪ ✪ This branch of the Victoria and Albert Museum has outstanding collections of toys, games, dolls and dolls' houses; also children's costume; many activities for children. The local history collection includes displays of Spitalfields silk. Open: weekdays 10 a.m. to 5.30 p.m. Sun. 2.30 to 5.30 p.m. Closed Fridays, Good Fri., Christmas Eve and Day and Boxing Day.

Station: Bethnal Green. Cen.

■ **Big Ben.** Westminster. 1C 94 ✪✪✪ Although popularly used to describe the clock tower, Big Ben is in fact the name of the 13½ ton bell which strikes the hours. It was cast at the Whitechapel Foundry in 1858. The tower stands 320 feet. *Station:* Westminster. Cir.D.J.

■ **Billingsgate,** Lower Thames Street. 2B 86 The name of London's oldest market, it was restricted in the 17th century to dealing in fish. The 1874 Market Hall

4

facade is incorporated into the redeveloped site following the removal of trading to the Isle of Dogs in 1982.
*Stations:* Monument Cir.D., Tower Hill Cir.D.

■ **Bomber Command Museum.** See Outer London. ✪ ✪

■ **Bond Street.** 1C 80
The upper end which runs into Oxford Street is New Bond Street, and the lower end which runs into Piccadilly is Old Bond Street. This expensive London shopping street ranks in world fame with the Rue de la Paix in Paris, and New York's Fifth Avenue.
*Stations:* Bond Street Cen.J., Green Park J.P.V.

■ **Bramah Tea & Coffee Museum,** Maguire Street. 5E 87
Shows the history of the tea and coffee trade, including a collection of over 1000 tea pots and coffee makers.
*Admission Charge.* Open: daily 10 a.m. to 6 p.m.
*Stations:* London Bridge J.N. Tower Hill Cir.D.

■ **British Airways London Eye,** see London Eye ✪✪ ✪

■ **British Library,** 96 Euston Road. 3A 62 ✪✪✪
The worlds leading resource for scholorship and research, its new climate controlled building has 11 reading rooms, seating for 1200 researchers and nearly 12 million volumes stored in 4 levels of basements.   The public exhibition rooms include The Treasures Gallery housing some 200 of the most famous items including Lindisfarne Gospels, Magna Carta, Anglo-Saxon Chronicle, Gutenburg Bible, Shakespeare's First Folio, Nelson's log books, Scott's Antarctic Journal.
*Admission.* **Treasures Gallery and Public areas, cafe, bookshop** open Mon, Wed, Thurs, Fri: 9.30 a.m. to 6 p.m. Tues: to 8 p.m.  Sat. to 5 p.m.  Sun. 11 a.m. to 5 p.m. (*Reading Rooms* open to ticket holders only for research that cannot be carried out elsewhere).
Closed Christmas, and New Year.
*Station:* King's Cross St. Pancras. Cir.D.M.N.P.V.

■ **British Museum,** Great Russell Street. 3A 70 ✪✪✪ ✪
Originally founded in 1753 from several private collections this rapidly became the finest Museum in existence. Its unrivalled collections are comprised in the Departments of Coins and Medals, Egyptian Antiquities, Western Asiatic Antiquities, Greek and Roman Antiquities, (including the famous Elgin Marbles), British and Medieval Antiquities Oriental Antiquities and Prints and Drawings
    The famous former reading room is now the centrepiece of the restored inner courtyard, a spectacular covered public square 'The Great Court' (Opens Dec. 2000), with restaurants, museum shops, education facilities; giving access both through the museum and between the surrounding galleries.

Open: weekdays 10 a.m. to 5 p.m.; Sun. 12.00 to 6 p.m.
Closed: Christmas Eve and Day, Boxing Day and Good
Friday, New Year's Day. Free lectures on certain days.
*Stations*: Russell Square P., Tottenham Court Road C.N.

■ **Buckingham Palace,** The Mall, 1C 92  ✪✪✪
London Palace of Her Majesty Queen Elizabeth II. When
she is in residence the Royal Standard flies from the mast,
at other times the Union Flag is flown. Changing of the
Guard takes place daily at 11.30 a.m. on certain days, see
*Pageantry* for details. Built by the Duke of Buckingham in
1703. Buckingham Palace was bought by George III in
1761, was rebuilt again by George IV, and became Queen
Victoria's London home. Refaced in 1913. The Queen's
Gallery, which forms part of the private chapel destroyed
in the Second World War, contains a varying exhibition of
masterpieces and works of art from the royal art treasures.
STATE ROOMS Open: During August and September by
timed ticket only, ticket office in Green Park 5D 81. For
details Tel: 020 7799 2331  Admission Charge.
QUEEN'S GALLERY  Closed for enlarging until 2002.
ROYAL MEWS  Open: 10.30am to 4.30 pm in Aug.& Sept.
Then 12 to 4 p.m. Wed. only Oct. to March. Tues. Wed. &
Thurs. March to early Aug. Admission Charge. *Stations:*
Green Park J.P.V., St. James's Park Cir.D., Victoria Cir.D.V.

■ **Cabinet War Rooms,** King Charles Street. 5A 82  ✪
One of the Second World War bunkers used by Winston
Churchill and his staff. On display are the cabinet office
central map room, Churchill's office and bedroom, the
transatlantic telephone room; all restored to their wartime
appearance.
*Admission Charge*. Open: 9.30 a.m. to 6 p.m April to Sept.
10am. to 6pm. Oct. to Mar. *Station:* Westminster. Cir.D.J.

■ **\*Camden Lock Market,** Camden High Street, N1
A popular lively street market on Sat. and Sun. in an
interesting canalside setting; clothes, crafts, antiques etc.
*Station:* Camden Town. N.

■ **\*Camden Passage,** N1  *Station:* Angel N.
A popular centre for antique arcades and shops.

■ **\*Carlyle's House,** 24 Cheyne Row, SW3
The famous writer lived here from 1834 until his death in
1881. The house has hardly been altered since. Now a
National Trust property.
*Admission Charge*. Open: April to October 11 a.m. to 4.30
p.m. Wed. to Sun. Closed Mon. and Tues.; and November
to March.  *Station:* Sloane Square Cir.D.

■ **Carnaby Street.** 5D 69
Popular teenage fashion centre of the late 1960's.
*Stations:*  Oxford Circus B. Cen. V., Piccadilly Circus B.P.

**Cenotaph, The,** Whitehall. 5B 82
Designed by Sir Edwin Lutyens, it now stands as a perpetual memorial to 'The Glorious Dead' of both World Wars. On the Sunday nearest November 11th of each year, crowds gather at the Cenotaph for the two minutes silence, and wreaths are laid by the Queen, members of the Government and other mourners.
*Stations:* Charing Cross B.N., Westminster Cir.D.J.

**Central Criminal Court,** Old Bailey. 4B 72
Known as 'The Old Bailey', the present building was completed in 1907 on the site of Newgate Prison. The lofty tower is surmounted by a bronze gilt figure of Justice. During important trials in Court 1, a large crowd gathers outside in the hope of gaining admission to the Public Gallery in Newgate Street, which seats 28. Five other courts seat up to 32 each. Open: 10.30-1pm., 2- 4.30 pm. No children under 14 admitted. *Station:* St. Paul's Cen.

**Central Hall,** Tothill Street 1A 94
This large domed building is the Methodists' London Headquarters. It is often used for conferences, exhibitions and concerts. The first session of the General Assembly of the United Nations took place here in 1946.
*Stations:* Westminster Cir.D.J.  St. James's Park Cir.D.

**\*Chelsea Physic Garden,** 66 Royal Hospital Road. SW3
Botanic gardens established in 1673 for the propagation and study of new species, from which several staple industries in former British colonies were derived.
*Admission Charge.* Open: Easter to Oct. 2 pm. to  5 p.m. Wed. and 2 pm. to 6 pm. Sun.  Entrance in Swan Walk.
*Station:* Sloane Square Cir.D.

**Cheshire Cheese,** Ye Olde.  Wine Office Court, 145 Fleet Street. 4A 72
An old and little-altered inn, famous for its Pudding, served at lunch times between Oct. and April. Tradition has it that Dr. Johnson Boswell and Oliver Goldsmith were habitues. Built in 1667 over cellars dating back to 1538.
Open: Bar daily Mon. to Sat. Restaurant Lunch daily, Dinner Mon. to Sat.  *Station:* Blackfriars Cir.D.

**Chinatown.** 1A 82
A lively centre of oriental sights, sounds and aromas, complete with chinese style gateways and telephone boxes. Between Shaftesbury Avenue and Leicester Square.  *Station:* Leicester Square N. P.

**Christie's,** 8 King Street. 3E 81
Is greatly reputed for its auction sales of valuable paintings furniture, silver, jewels, etc. held regularly. Telephone 020 7839 9060 for details.
*Station:* Green Park J.P.V.

■ **Clarence House,** St. James's Palace. 5E 81
The London residence of the Queen Mother.
*Station:* Green Park J.P.V.

■ **Cleopatra's Needle,** Victoria Embankment. 3D 83 ✪
An Egyptian obelisk which, about 3,500 years ago, stood in front of the Temple of the Sun at Heliopolis. When it was being towed to England in 1877, this 'Needle', $68^1/2$ feet high and weighing 180 tons, had to be abandoned in the Bay of Biscay during a storm. Its sister column is sited in Central Park, New York. *Station:* Embankment B.Cir.D.N.

■ **Clink Exhibition,** The Clink Prison, 1 Clink Street. 3F 85
Illustrates the infamous low life of this area, once known as 'The Liberty of the Clink'. Admission Charge.
Open: daily 10 a.m. to 10 p.m. Summer months. 10 a.m. to 6 p.m. Winter months. *Station:* London Bridge J.N.

■ **Clore Gallery,** see Tate Gallery.

■ **College of Arms,** or Heralds College, Queen Victoria Street. 1D 85   Deals with all matters relating to Heraldry genealogy and State Ceremonials and consists of three Kings of Arms (Garter, Clarenceux, and Norroy & Ulster), six Heralds and four Pursuivants, appointed by the Sovereign. The building, Derby House, reconstructed after the Great Fire, was presented to the College by Queen Mary I (Mary Tudor) in 1554.   The panelled Earl Marshal's Court is open 10 a.m. to 4 p.m. Mon. to Fri. (also open for heraldic and genealogical enquiries).
*Stations:* Blackfriars Cir.D. Mansion House Cir. D.

■ **\*Commonwealth Institute,** Kensington High Street, W8
Resource centre and reference library for Commonwealth studies. Public space for exhibitions, events and educational activities.
*Station:* Kensington High Street Cir.D.

■ **County Hall,** Westminster Bridge. 5D 75
Once housed the London County Council also the Greater London Council (G.L.C.) until 1986. Now home to the London Aquarium, FA Premier League Hall of Fame, restaurants, hotels and other leisure facilities. *Stations:* Waterloo B.J.N., Westminster Cir.D.J.

■ **Court Dress Collection,** see Kensington Palace.

■ **Courtauld Institute Galleries,** Somerset House. 1D 83
✪✪ Contains collections belonging to the University of London, and includes the Courtauld Collection of Impressionist and Post-Impressionist masterpieces by Manet, Renoir, Van Gogh and Cezanne.
*Admission Charge.* (Free on Mondays 10am. to 2pm.)
Open: Mon to Sat. 10 a.m. to 6 p.m. Sun. and Bank Holidays 12.00 to 6 p.m. . Closed Christmas and Jan 1st.

■ **Covent Garden,** Southampton Street, WC2. 1C 82 ✪✪
Originally 'Convent Garden' the square is now
pedestrianised with the central market hall restored and
open as an environment of shops, studios, cafes;
promenades and paved areas are venues for lively street
theatre.    The Flower Market now houses the London
Transport Museum and Theatre Museum.
The market given Royal Charter in 1671 grew into
London's largest wholesale fruit, vegetable and flower
market and has moved to a new site off Nine Elms Lane.
*Station:* Covent Garden P

■ **Craft Gallery,** 44a Pentonville Road. 2F 63
The Crafts Council showcase for artist-craftsmen,
changing exhibitions throughout the year. Craftsman
Index, slide Library research facilities. Open 11 a.m. to 6
p.m. Tues. to Sat. 2 p.m. to 6 p.m. Sun.    *Station:* Angel N.

■ **Crafts Centre,** Institute of Contemporary Applied Arts,
2 Percy Street, 3F 69        Federation of British Craft
Societies mount fine exhibitions of work by artist-
craftsmen. Open 10.30 a.m. to 5.30 p.m. Mon. to Sat.
*Station:* Tottenham Court Road Cen. N.

■ **Custom House,** Lower Thames Street. 2B 86
Until 1940, the headquarters of the Commissioners of
Customs and Excise. This has been the approximate site
of successive Custom Houses from the 14th century. The
Commissioners are now at New Kings Beam House, Upper
Ground, SE2. *Stations:* Monument Cir.D. Tower Hill Cir.D.

■ **Cutty Sark,** see Outer London. ✪✪✪ ✪

■ **Dali Universe,** County Hall. 5D 83
Exhibition of artworks by the Spanish surrealist Salvador
Dali, including sculptures, graphics and watercolours.
*Admission Charge.* Open: 10.am to 5.30 pm. daily.
*Stations:* Waterloo B.J.N. Westminster Cir.D. J.

■ **Design Museum,** Shad Thames. 5E 87
Covers the history, practice, theory and future of design in
mass-produced consumer products and services.
*Admission Charge.* Open: 11.30 a.m. to 6 p.m. Mon. to
Fri.12.00 to 6 p.m. Sat & Sun.
*Stations:* London Bridge J.N. Tower Hill Cir.D.

■ **Dickens House,** 48 Doughty Street. 1E 71
Although the author lived here only from 1837 to 1839,
'Oliver Twist' and 'Nicholas Nickelby' were written and the
'Pickwick Papers' completed during those two years. The
house is now a Museum of Dickens Memorabilia, and the
headquarters of the Dickens Fellowship.
*Admission Charge.* Open: 10a.m. to 5p.m. Closed

Sundays and Bank Holidays. *Station:* Russell Square P.

■ **Dirty Dick's,** 202 Bishopsgate. 3C 74
The present tavern, owes its name to an 18th-century tragedy. Nathaniel Bentley, a wealthy dandy, heard of the death of his bride-to-be on the day they were to celebrate their engagement. From then on he took no care of his appearance or of his house which became known as 'Dirty Dick's. *Station:* Liverpool Street Cen.Cir.M.

■ **Doctor Johnson's House,** 17 Gough Square. 4A 72
The famous 18th-century writer immortalised by Boswell, lived here from 1748 to 1759. The house contains an early edition of his Dictionary which was compiled here and published in 1755 selling for four guineas. Here also he wrote 'The Rambler' which appeared twice weekly for two years with a circulation of about five hundred.
*Admission Charge.* Open: Weekdays 11 a.m. to 5.30 p.m. (Oct. to April 5 p.m.). Closed Sundays and Bank Holidays. *Station:* Blackfriars Cir.D.

■ **Downing Street,** Whitehall. 5B 82 ✪
No.10 Downing Street is world-famous as the home of the British Prime Minister and the scene of Cabinet meetings. No. 11 houses the Chancellor of the Exchequer, and No. 12 is the Government Whip's office.
*Station:* Westminster Cir.D.J.

■ **Duke of York's Column,** Waterloo Place. 4F 81 ✪
This column, which stands above the steps leading to St. James's Park, is 124 feet high, and was erected in 1833 as a memorial to Frederick, Duke of York, the second son of George III. Although an able and devoted Army administrator, as Commander-in-Chief he was less successful in the field: according to popular song he 'led his ten thousand men up a hill and then he led them down again'!
*Stations:* Piccadilly Circus B.P., Charing Cross B.N.

■ **\*Earl's Court,** Warwick Road, SW5
Large exhibition halls for national events and important shows. The Royal Tournament is held here annually.
*Stations:* Earls Court D.P., West Kensington D.

■ **Ely Place.** 3A 72
The site of Ely Palace, London home of the Bishops of Ely in which John of Gaunt died in 1399. Demolished in 1772 it is now a private cul-de-sac of 18th century houses still watched over by a beadle at the gated entrance. The only remains are Ely Chapel or St. Etheldreda's Church the first pre-Reformation Church to be restored to Roman Catholic worship. *Station:* Farringdon Cir.M.

■ **Eros,** see Piccadilly Circus. ✪✪✪

■ **Faraday Museum,** Royal Institution, 20 Albemarle Street
2D 81    Devoted to Michael Faraday's work and life
including his own laboratory and equipment.
*Admission Charge.* Open 10 a.m. to 6 p.m. Mon. to Fri.
*Station:* Green Park J.P.V..

■ **Fleet Street. 5F 71**
Traditionally, but no longer the centre of the British
newspaper industry, following the introduction of modern
technology in new premises mainly on redeveloped
dockland sites.    *Stations:* Temple Cir.D., Blackfriars Cir.D.

■ **Florence Nightingale Museum,** Lambeth Palace Road,
1D 95    Illustrates the life and work of this famous woman,
including a life size reconstruction of a ward at the Crimea.
*Admission Charge.* Open: 10 a.m. to 4 p.m. Tues to Sun.
*Stations:* Westminster Cir.D.J. Waterloo B.J.N.

■ **Football Association Hall of Fame,** Westminster Bridge
Road, 1D95    Experience the spirit of English football from
the past, present and into the future, and capture the
passion in this celebration of the national game.
*Admission Charge.* Open: 10 am. to 6pm. daily.
*Stations:* Westminster Cir.D.J. Waterloo B.J.N.

■ **\*Geffrye Museum,** Kingsland Road, E2.
Housed in Almshouses erected in 1915 by the
Ironmongers' Company. It comprises a series of period
rooms dating from the 16th to the 20th century, containing
furniture, domestic equipment and musical instruments
from middle class homes.
Open: 10 a.m. to 5 p.m.; Sun. 2 to 5 p.m. Closed Mondays,
(except Bank Holiday Mon).    *Station:* Old Street N.

■ **Gilbert Collection,** Somerset House. 1E 83 ✪
Magnificent decorative arts collection, 800 items including
European silver, gold snuff boxes and Italian mosaics.
*Admission Charge.* Open: 10 am. to 6 pm. Mon. to Sat.
12.00 to 6 pm. Sun. and Bank Holidays. Closed Christmas,
Jan. 1st.    *Station:* Temple Cir.D., Charing Cross N.B.

■ **Golden Hinde,** St Mary Overie Dock, Cathedral Street.
3F 85 ✪    Floating museum ship, a full scale, ocean-going
reconstruction of Sir Francis Drake's famous galleon.
*Admission Charge.* Open: 10 a.m to 6 p.m. (4 pm winter),
unless closed for functions.    *Station:* London Bridge J.N.

■ **Goldsmiths' Hall,** Foster Lane. 4D 73
Home of the Goldsmiths' Company, one of the twelve
Great Livery Companies of the City of London. Since 1281
a jury containing several goldsmiths has been responsible
for the Trial of the Pyx, the testing of newly minted coins,
and from 1870 this has been held annually at Goldsmiths
Hall.    Gold and silver are assayed and hallmarked here,

but the Assay Office is not open to the public. The Company possesses one of the most representative collections of antique plate in the country, a notable example being the coronation cup of Queen Elizabeth I. *Station:* St. Paul's Cen.

■ **Gray's Inn,** High Holborn. 2E 71 ✪
One of the four great Inns of Court. The historic Elizabethan Hall has been fully restored since the war. The Chapel also suffered damage by bombing. Francis Bacon, who was a student of the Inn, is said to have planted the catalpa tree in the gardens. *Station:* Chancery Lane Cen. (closed Sundays). Holborn Cen. P.

■ **Green Park.** 4C 80 ✪
Covers an area of 53 acres. The fine iron gateway on the Piccadilly side is that of old Devonshire House.
*Stations:* Green Park J.P.V., Hyde Park Corner P.

■ **Greenwich,** see Outer London. ✪✪✪ ✪

■ **Guard's Chapel,** see Guards Museum.

■ **Guards Museum,** Birdcage Walk. 1E 93
Illustrates the 300-year history of the Brigade of Guards. Adjacent is Guard's Chapel, rebuilt 1963 incorporating surviving apse of the earlier chapel devastated 1944 by a flying bomb during a morning service with the loss of 121 lives.    *Admission Charge.* Open 10 a.m. to 4 p.m. daily
*Station:* St James's Park Cir.D.

■ **Guildhall,** Gresham Street. 4F 73 ✪
Has been the centre of civic government in the City of London for more than a thousand years. It dates from 1411-39. The original building, except the porch, the crypt with its lovely vaulting, and the structure of the Hall, was destroyed in the Great Fire of 1666. The Great Hall is used for the Presentation of the Freedom of the City and other civic functions. Here the Livery Companies, twelve of whose banners hang from the walls, annually elect the new Lord Mayor and Sheriffs. The Lord Mayor's procession is held on the second Saturday in November and the banquet the following Monday.
Modern extensions contain the Guildhall Library, including the Clockmaker's Company Museum, the Corporation of London Record Office—regarded as the most complete collection of ancient municipal records in existence, also the Guildhall Art Gallery showing the collection of the Corporation of London—particularly rich in Victorian Art.
Open: GUILDHALL (Subject to functions), Summer 10 am to 5 pm Mon. to Fri. 10 to 4 pm Sat. and Sun. Closed Sun. in Winter.  LIBRARY & RECORD OFFICE 9.30 am to 5 pm. Mon. to Sat. closed Sun.  (Record Office closed Sat. & Sun.).  MUSEUM 9.30 am to 4.45 pm Mon. to Fri. only.

GALLERY 10am. to 5 pm. Mon. to Sat. 12.00 to 4pm. Sun. (Admission charge). *Station:* Bank Cen.N

■ **Hampton Court Palace,** see Outer London ✪✪✪

■ **Hatton Garden,** Holborn. 2A 72
Stands partly on the site of the old palace of the Bishop of Ely. It is well known as an important centre of the world's diamond trade. *Station:* Farringdon Cir.H.M.

■ **Hayward Gallery,** Belvedere Road, South Bank. 4E 83 ✪
Changing shows of either modern art, a historical theme or international loan exhibitions. *Admission Charge.*
Open 10 a.m. to 6 p.m. daily during exhibitions.
*Stations:* Embankment B.Cir.D. Waterloo B.J.N.

■ **H.M.S. Belfast.** See "Belfast". ✪✪ ✪

■ **Hermitage Rooms,** Somerset House. 1E 83 ✪
An exhibition of treasures from the Hermitage Museum of St. Petersburg providing a unique window on Russian art and history. Due to open end Nov. 2000. *Admission charge.* Open 10 a.m. to 6 p.m. Mon. to Sat. 12.00 to 6 pm. Sun. and Bank Hols. Closed Christmas and Jan 1st. *Stations:* Temple Cir.D., Charing Cross N.B.

■ **Horse Guards,** Whitehall. 4B 82 ✪✪✪ ✪
These barracks were rebuilt in 1753. Two mounted guardsmen are on sentry duty here, and the Changing of the Guard daily at 11 a.m., Sundays 10 a.m., is a picturesque sight. Trooping the Colour, a magnificent ceremony, takes place on the Queen's official birthday on the parade ground at the rear of the building.
*Stations:* Embankment B.Cir.D. Charing Cross B.N.

■ **Houses of Parliament,** Parliament Square. 1C 94 ✪✪✪
Stand throughout the world as a symbol of democratic government. Rebuilt in 1840 on the site of the Old Palace of Westminster, which was destroyed by fire, this is the largest building erected in England since the Reformation. When Parliament sits, a flag flies from Victoria Tower by day, and by night a light shines high in the famous 'Big Ben' clock tower.     For admission to hear debates apply to an M.P.; or join the public queue for the Stranger's Gallery outside St. Stephen's Entrance . For current tours information telephone House of Commons Information Office on 020 7219 4272   *Station:* Westminster Cir.D.J.

■ **Hyde Park.** 3B 78 ✪✪
This Royal Park covers 341 acres, and together with Kensington Gardens forms an oasis of green tranquillity. On Sundays the park is crowded, and it is then that the famous 'tub-thumping' public orators on rostrums and soap boxes air their views to groups of listeners at Speaker's Corner, near Marble Arch. The Serpentine, a large lake in the centre of the park, provides boating, and

13

is one of London's Lidos (open from the last Saturday in April until the second Sunday in October).
*Stations:* Hyde Park Corner P., Knightsbridge P., Lancaster Gate Cen., Marble Arch Cen.

■ **Imperial War Museum,** Lambeth Road. 3A 96 ✪✪✪ ✪
Records and illustrates all aspects of warfare, military and civil, allied and enemy, in which Britain and the Commonwealth have been involved since August 1914. Besides the machinery of war there are works of art, photographic and film records, printed materials and Holocaust Exhibition. Dramatic recreations include WW1 'Trench Experience' and WWII 'Blitz Experience' with sounds, smells and special effects.
*Admission Charge.* Open: 10 a.m. to 6 p.m. daily. (Free from 4.30 p.m. daily). Closed Christmas Eve and Day, Boxing Day, Good Friday, New Year's Day. Reference Dept. Mon. to Fri. 10 a.m. to 5 p.m. by appointment. Free lectures and films on certain days.
*Stations:* Lambeth North B., Elephant and Castle B.N.

■ **Jewish Museum,** 129/131 Albert Street. 1C 60
Contains antiquities in silver, wood, ivory, pottery and textiles illustrating Jewish domestic and public worship.
**Admission Charge.** Open: 10 a.m. to 4 p.m. Sun. to Thurs. Closed Fri. & Sat. Bank Hols. Jewish Festivals. Conducted tours of parties by prior appointment.
*Station:* Mornington Crescent N.

■ **Kensington Gardens.** 3D 77 ✪✪
Formerly the grounds of Kensington Palace, now a woodland park where children gather at the Round Pond to sail their boats, visit the statue of Peter Pan and explore the Diana, Princess of Wales Memorial Playground – the 7 mile long memorial walkway passes nearby. The Long Water should be seen from the bridge that divides it from the Serpentine. The Serpentine Gallery has changing and challenging exhibitions of modern art.
*Stations:* High Street Kensington Cir.D., Lancaster Gate Cen., Queensway Cen.

■ **Kensington Palace,** Kensington Gardens. 4C 76 ✪✪
Designed by Wren for William III, Queen Victoria was born here. The London home of Diana, Princess of Wales, until her untimely death in 1997. Two portions are open to the public, the 'State Rooms' and the 'Court Dress Collection'.
*Admission Charge.* Open: Daily 10 a.m. to 5 p.m. (last admission 4.15). Closed Christmas Eve and Day, Boxing Day, New Year's Day and Good Friday
*Stations:* High Street Kensington Cir.D., Queensway Cen.

■ **Kew Gardens,** see Outer London. ✪✪

■ **Knightsbridge. 1D 91** ✪
Famous area for high quality shopping, especially Harrods and Harvey Nichols. *Station:* Knightsbridge.

■ **Lambeth Palace,** Lambeth Palace Road. **3D 95**
Has been for over 700 years the London residence of the Archbishop of Canterbury. Of particular interest is the Library with its 1,700 manuscripts. Open: By appointment only. *Stations:* Westminster Cir.D.J., Lambeth North B.

■ **Lancaster House,** Stable Yard House. **5D 81**
This early Victorian mansion is known for the splendour of its State Apartments.
*Stations:* Green Park J.P.V., St. James's Park Cir.D.

■ **Leadenhall Market,** Leadenhall Street. **5B 74**
Victorian glass and Iron hall of 1881. Once specialised in poultry, now in quality delicatessen shops.
*Station:* Monument Cir.D.

■ **Leicester Square. 2A 82** ✪
Was laid out from 1635-70, and named after the Earl of Leicester, whose residence was on its north side. Hogarth and Joshua Reynolds also lived here.
*Station:* Leicester Square N.P.

■ **Lincoln's Inn,** Chancery Lane. **4E 71** ✪
One of the four inns of Court which have the power of 'calling to the Bar'. The Law Library, built in 1845, is the finest in London and contains over 70,000 volumes and many fine MSS. Of particular interest are the early 16th century gateway to Chancery Lane and the Inigo Jones chapel erected in 1623. *Admission:* To the Inn, on application. To the Chapel, free Sunday service 11.30 a.m., during sittings. *Stations:* Chancery Lane Cen. (closed Sundays), Holborn Cen.P.

■ **Lloyd's,** Lime Street. **5B 74**
This international insurance market and world centre of shipping intelligence is named after Edward Lloyd's coffee house, the 17th-century rendezvous of people interested in shipping. The famous Lutine Bell is rung when an announcement of special importance is to be made from the Rostrum, particularly with regard to overdue vessels. The exciting modern building has external observation lifts and service ducting in strong colours; the whole building being well and dramatically illuminated at night.
*Stations:* Aldgate Cir.N., Bank Cen.N. Monument Cir.D

■ **Lombard Street. 5A 74**
Famous as the centre of banking, it owes its name to the Jewish Lombard goldsmiths and money-lenders who established themselves here after their expulsion in 1290.
*Station:* Bank Cen.N.

■ **London Aquarium,** County Hall. 5D 83 ✪ ✪
One of Europe's largest exhibits of fish and marine life from around the world features Atlantic and Pacific Ocean tanks, European and Exotic habitats, touch pools. *Admission Charge.*Open daily.*Station:*Westminster Cir.D.J.

■ **London Bridge. 3A 86**
There have been many bridges on this site, the first having been built by the Romans. The present bridge replaced the 1831 stone bridge, now in Lake Havasu City, Arizona U.S.A.   *Stations:* London Bridge J.N. Monument Cir.D.

■ **London Bridge City. 3B 86** ✪
A traffic-free environment of offices, shops, apartments, restaurants, and leisure facilities. Incorporated are the Victorian Hay's Dock buildings now called Hay's Galleria, and a riverside walk with panoramic views of the 'City', access to HMS Belfast and linking London Bridge and Tower Bridge.   *Station:* London Bridge. J.N.

■ **London Canal Museum,** New Wharf Road. IC 62
Tells the story of London's canals, including the role of working horses; housed in what was an industrial ice house built in the 1850's for Carlo Gatti the ice cream manufacturer.   *Admission Charge.* Open: Tues. to Sun. 10 a.m. to 4.30 p.m.
*Station:* King's Cross, St. Pancras Cir.D.P.N.V.M.H.

■ **London Dungeon,** Tooley Street. 4A 86  ✪ ✪
An exhibition of gruesome and macabre events from the Dark Ages until the end of the 17th century, not recommended by the management to the nervous or unaccompanied children.   *Admission Charge.* Open: 7 days a week from 10 a.m. last admission 5 pm. Closes earlier in winter.   *Station:* London Bridge. J.N.

■ **London Eye,** County Hall, 5D 83 ✪✪✪ ✪
The world's highest observation wheel provides spectacular views over London from one of 32 enclosed capsules. Gradual 30 minute ride reaches 450ft above the River Thames.   *Admmission charge.* Open daily. *Stations:* Westminster Cir.D.J.  Waterloo B.J.N.

■ **London Pavilion,** see Piccadilly Circus.

■ **London Planetarium,** Marylebone Road. 1F 67  ✪✪✪ ✪
A vast hemispherical dome on which, by a £70,000 Zeiss projector, images of the celestial bodies are shown, accurate in size, brightness and position relative to each other, also their relative paths and speeds through the night sky. *Admission Charge.* Regular performances throughout the day. Open 10.20 to 5 pm. daily. Closed Christmas Day.   *Station:* Baker Street B.Cir.J.M.H.

■ **London Stone,** Cannon Street. 1F 85

This stone is believed to have been the millarium from which the Romans measured the distances out of the City. It was moved in 1798 to its present position.
*Station:* Cannon Street Cir.D. (closed Sundays)

■ **London Telecom Tower,** Maple Street. 2D 69
This 620 ft. structure was built to facilitate tele-communications without interference from other tall buildings.  *Stations:* Warren Street N.V., Goodge Street N

■ **London Transport Museum,** Covent Garden. 1C 82
✪✪✪ ✪ Historic vehicles and exhibits including early steam and electric locomotives, horse-buses, motor buses (including the famous 'B' type), tram cars, trolley buses, posters, tickets, signs, etc. Sit in the driving seat of a London Bus or Underground Train; historical films show London as it was. Housed in a magnificent Victorian structure with cast iron arcades and glazed clerestories.
*Admission Charge.* Open daily 10 a.m. to 6 p.m. Closed Christmas Day and Boxing Day  *Station:* Covent Garden P.

■ **London Zoo,** Regent's Park. 1F 59 ✪✪✪✪
The 'lure of the wild' in the heart of London; a day among the thousands of animals here (many of them endangered species), is a day with a difference. Special attractions include the 'Web of Life' combining animals and interactive displays explaining biological diversity, how it is threatened and how we can help to preseve it; conservation work in progress is displayed. The Aquarium, the walk-through Snowdon Aviary, Moonlight World where day and night are reversed, Penguin Pool—an essay in delicate curves, Bear Mountain, the Elephant House—a great concrete fortress, are other features. Theres a Childrens Zoo; various rides and animal encounters and animal feeding takes place at certain times.  *Admission Charge.* Open March to Oct. 10 a.m. to 5.30 p.m. Nov. to Feb. 10 a.m. to 4.30 p.m.
*Stations:* Camden Town N. Regent's Park B.

■ **Madame Tussaud's,** Marylebone Road. 1F 67 ✪✪✪✪
The world-famous waxwork exhibition and tourist attraction, where visitors wander among themed displays featuring life-like historical, showbiz and contemporary figures. *Admission Charge.* Open: 10 a.m. to 5.30 p.m. Mon. to Fri. 9.30 a.m. to 5.30 p.m. Sat. & Sun. Closed only on Christmas Day.  *Station:* Baker Street B.Cir.J.M.H

■ **Mansion House.** 5F 73
This, the first official residence of the Lord Mayors of London, was built in 1753. Until this time the Mayors had to receive in their own homes. The famous banquets given by the Lord Mayor take place in the Egyptian Hall. The Mansion House Justice Room is in the same building.

*Station:* Bank Cen.N.

■ **Marble Arch,** Oxford Street. 1E 79
Originally intended as an entrance to Buckingham Palace, this 'triumphal arch' was made too narrow for the State Coach and was utilised as a gate into Hyde Park. Later, the park boundary was moved back, leaving Marble Arch an entrance to nowhere. Nearby, where Edgware Road intersects Bayswater Road, stood Tyburn Gallows, where public executions took place until 1783.
*Station:* Marble Arch Cen.

■ **Marlborough House,** Pall Mall. 4F 81
Built by Wren in 1709 for the Duke of Marlborough, it reverted to the Crown in 1817. Amongst its occupants have been Edward VII when Prince of Wales, and George V until his accession. From 1911 until her death it was the residence of Queen Alexandra. Queen Mary lived here when in London. Now a Commonwealth Conference Centre.
Adjoining the house is QUEEN'S CHAPEL 1627, designed by Inigo Jones. Services: Sun 8.30 and 11.15 a.m. Easter Day—end of July.   *Station:* Green Park J.P.V.

■ **Middlesex Guildhall,** Broad Sanctuary. 1A 94
The former County Hall built by J. S. Gibson 1905-13, it stands on the site of the old belfry of Westminster Abbey.
*Station:* Westminster Cir.D.J.

■ **Monument, The.** 1A 86 ✪
A fluted Doric column erected by Sir Christopher Wren in the year 1677 to commemorate the Great Fire of London of 1666. Its height is 202 feet, which is the distance to the house in Pudding Lane where the fire broke out.
The magnificent view of the City from the top well repays the effort of ascending the 311 steps.
*Admission Charge.* Open daily 10 am. to 6 pm. (last admission 5.40 pm.). Closed Good Friday, Christmas Day and Boxing Day.
*Station:* Monument Cir.D.

■ **Museum of Childhood,** see Bethnal Green.

■ **Museum of Garden History,** Lambeth Palace Road. 3D 95.    Formed by the Tradescant Trust in the restored St. Mary-at-Lambeth church in honour of the Tradescants— gardeners to Charles I, and responsible for the introduction of many exotic plants into England. Voluntary contributions appreciated.
Open Mon. to Fri. 10.30 a.m. to 4 p.m. Sun. 10.30 a.m. to 5 p.m. Closed Sat. Closed mid December to March. *Station:* Westminster Cir.D.J.

■ **Museum of London,** London Wall. 3D 73 ✪ ✪

One of London's modern purpose-built museums: constructed as part of the Barbican it is designed to lead visitor's through the chronological development of London and environs from prehistoric times to the present day. Imaginative displays and excellent facilities earned it Museum of the Year award 1978. *Admission Charge.*
Open: Mon. to Sat. 10 a.m. to 5.50 p.m. Sun. 12.00 to 5.50 p.m. Closed Christmas and Boxing Day. Free lectures on certain days.
*Stations:* Barbican Cir.M.H. (closed Sun.) St. Paul's Cen

◼ **Museum of Methodism**, see Wesley's House.

◼ **Museum of the Moving Image.** Closed until further notice.

◼ **\*National Army Museum,** Royal Hospital Road, Chelsea. SW3. ✪ Museum of the British Army, and of the Indian Army to 1947 also colonial and auxiliary forces.
Open: 10 a.m. to 5.30 p.m. daily. Closed Good Friday, Christmas Eve and Day, Boxing Day and New Year's Day.
*Station:* Sloane Square Cir.D.

◼ **National Gallery,** Trafalgar Square. 2A 82 ✪✪✪
The Gallery was opened in 1824 with the Angerstein Collection of 38 pictures has become one of the most important picture galleries in the world, containing a collection representative of every European school of painting and works by nearly all the Great Masters.
In addition special exhibitions of great interest are mounted throughout the year.
Open: 10 a.m. to 6 p.m.; Wed. to 9 p.m.; Sundays 12 noon to 6 p.m., Closed Christmas Eve and Day, Boxing Day and Good Friday. Free lectures on certain days.
*Station:* Charing Cross B.N.

◼ **National Maritime Museum,** see Outer London. ✪✪✪✪

◼ **National Portrait Gallery,** St. Martin's Place. 2A 82 ✪
National collection of painted and photographic portraits of famous British men and women dating mainly from the Tudor dynasty to the twentieth century.
Open: 10 a.m. to 6 p.m. Mon. to Sat. Thurs. and Fri. to 9pm. Sundays 12 to 6 p.m. Closed Good Friday, Christmas and Boxing Day. *Stations:* Leicester Square N.P., Charing Cross B.N.

◼ **National Postal Museum,** Closed until further notice.

◼ **National Theatre,** see South Bank Arts Centre

◼ **Natural History Museum,** Cromwell Rd. 3F 89 ✪✪✪✪
One of the world's finest collections of natural history and earth sciences (including the galleries of the former Geological Museum). As well as the traditional displays e.g. Zoology, Entomology, Palaeontology, rocks, minerals and fossils (including moon rock), the museum features

new stimulating visual learn-and-enjoy style exhibitions including Hall of Human Biology, Man's Place in Evolution, Introducing Ecology, Dinosaurs and Their Living Relatives, Origin of Species, British Natural History, The Power Within (earthquakes and volcanoes), Visions of Earth, Restless Surface. Activity sheets available for children.
*Admission Charge.* Open: 10 a.m. to 5.50 p.m.; Sun. 11.00 a.m. to 5.50 p.m. Free after 4.30pm (5pm Sat. Sun. and Bank Hols.) Closed Christmas Eve and Day, Boxing Day and Good Friday. *Station:* South Kensington Cir.D.P.

■ **New Scotland Yard,** Broadway. 2F 93
The Headquarters of the Metropolitan Police and of its Criminal Investigation Department. Formerly situated on Victoria Embankment. Admission: visiting police officers only. *Station:* St. James's Park Cir. D

■ **\*Olympia,** Hammersmith Road, W14.
It covers an area of 103/4 acres, and is one of the most famous showplaces and exhibition centres in the world.
*Station:* Kensington (Olympia) D. (Exhibitions only.)

■ **Operating Theatre Museum,** 9a St. Thomas' St. 4F 85
An original Victorian operating theatre, with instruments, apparatus and Herb Garret. *Admission Charge.*
Open: 10 a.m. to 4 p.m. daily. *Station:* London Bridge J.N.

■ **Oratory, The,** Brompton Road. 3B 90 ✪
Built in the Italian Renaissance style during the 19th century, it is well known for its fine musical services. Cardinal Newman served here as priest after his conversion from the Anglican to the Roman Catholic faith.
Open: 6 a.m. to 8 p.m. daily.
*Station:* South Kensington Cir.D.P.

■ **Oxford Street.** 5B 68 ✪
One of Londons principal shopping streets, famous for its many department stores including Selfridges, John Lewis, Debenhams. Remarkably straight for London, it is on the site of the old Roman road leading west from the city.
*Stations:* Bond Street Cen.J., Marble Arch Cen., Oxford Circus B. Cen.V., Tottenham Court Road Cen.N.

■ **Oxo Tower Wharf,** South Bank 2A 84 ✪
A South Bank landmark, this imposing wharf is now a showpiece centre for artist designer-craftsmen; rooftop restaurant and 8th floor public viewing gallery.
See also Gabriel's Wharf nearby.
*Stations:* Waterloo B. J.N. Blackfriars Cir.D. Southwark J.

■ **'Petticoat Lane',** Middlesex Street. 3D 75 ✪
A street market for a numerous variety of goods where on Sunday mornings, bargain-hunters and passers-by are attracted to the stalls of persuasive salesmen.

*Stations:* Aldgate East D.M., Liverpool Street Cen.Cir.M.

■ **Photographers Gallery,** 5 Gt. Newport Street, Off Charing Cross Road.  1A 82
Changing exhibitions by living photographers and pictures from the past; bookshop and print sales.  Open 11 a.m. to 6 p.m. Mon. to Sat.  12.00 to 6 pm. Sun.  *Station:* Leicester Square N.P.

■ **Piccadilly Circus.** 2F 81 ✪✪✪
A swirl of people, traffic and coloured lights; this is the traditional focal point of London.  A pedestrian piazza links the famous Eros statue to the south side; both the Trocadero Centre and the London Pavilion provide traffic free environments of shopping and leisure facilities—see also Rock Circus and Segaworld.
*Station:* Piccadilly Circus B.P.

■ **Pollocks Toy Museum,** 1 Scala Street. 3E 69  ✪
Of particular interest to children of all ages. Toy theatres, games dolls, dolls' houses and toys, etc.
*Admission Charge.* Open: 10 a.m. to 5 p.m. Mon. to Sat. Closed Sun.; Christmas and Boxing Days and Easter Mon.
*Station:* Goodge Street N.

■ **\*Portobello Road Market,** Portobello Road, W11. ✪
Famous for its Saturday market of antiques, Victoriana, pseudo-antiques, but the rest of the week Portobello and the surrounding streets are a lively mix of general market stalls, exotic food shops, fashion shops and restaurants.
*Station:* Ladbroke Grove M., Westbourne Park M.

■ **Post Office Tower,** see London Telecom Tower.

■ **Public Record Office,** See Outer London.

■ **Queen's Gallery,** see Buckingham Palace.  ✪

■ **Queen Victoria Memorial,** The Mall. 5D 81 ✪
Stands in front of Buckingham Palace. Of white marble the centre figure of the Queen is 13 ft high. Groups on the remaining sides represent Justice, Truth and Motherhood while the whole is surmounted by a winged Victory.
*Stations:* St. James's Park Cir.D. Victoria Cir.D.V. Green Park J.P.V.

■ **Regent's Park,** 2E 59 ✪✪
One of the largest London parks, this Royal Park covers an area of 472 acres and contains the Zoo and a large boating lake. Queen Mary's Gardens are famous for roses and the open-air theatre. The elegant terraces surrounding the Park by John Nash are now well contrasted by two modern buildings, the Royal College of Physicians and the London Central Mosque.
*Stations:* Baker Street B.Cir.J.M., Regent's Park B.

**Regent Street.** 1D 81 🟢

This important shopping street was first designed by Nash in 1813 as a link between Carlton House and Regent's Park. It is now famous for its quality shops, and department stores like Liberty and the toy emporium Hamleys.

*Stations:* Oxford Circus B.Cen.V., Piccadilly Circus B.P.

**Rock Circus,** see Trocadero. 🟢

**Roosevelt Memorial,** Grosvenor Square. 1A 80

Britain's personal memorial to President Franklin D. Roosevelt after the Second World War. 160,000 contributions of five shillings each closed the subscription list in less than 6 days. *Station:* Bond Street Cen.J.

**Royal Academy of Arts,** Burlington House, Piccadilly. 2E 81 🟢🟢 Founded by George III in 1768, the first President being Sir Joshua Reynolds. Varied special exhibitions of great interest are held throughout the year, incuding the annual Summer Exhibition of works by living artists, the private view of which is the first event of the London 'Season'. Gallery Shop and Framing Service.
*Admission Charge.* Open: 10 a.m. to 6 p.m. daily, to 8.30 pm. Fri. *Stations:* Piccadilly Circus B.P., Green Park J.P.V.

**Royal Air Force Museum,** See Outer London. 🟢🟢🟢 🟢

**Royal Albert Hall,** Kensington Gore. 1F 89 🟢

This largest Concert Hall in London, seating over 5,000 was completed in 1871. Home of the famous annual season of BBC Proms concerts.
*Station:* South Kensington Cir. D.P.

**Royal College of Music,** Prince Consort Road. 2F 89

Contains the Donaldson Musical Instrument collection of rare instruments with specimens of most of the early keyboard, stringed and wind instruments. Here also is the acclaimed Britten Opera Theatre opened 1987.
Open: Wed 2 to 4.30 p.m. in term time. Parties by appointment only, with the Curator only.
*Station:* South Kensington Cir.D.P.

**Royal College of Surgeons,** Lincoln's Inn Fields, 4E 71

Is the headquarters of surgery in England. Teaching, research and examinations are major functions of the College which contains within its medical museum the Hunter Collection. Open to members of the medical profession and to others on application to the Secretary.
*Station:* Holborn Cen.P.

**Royal Courts of Justice,** Strand, WC2. 5E 71

These buildings were opened in 1882, enlarged in 1911 and extended in 1968 and 1971. There are 50 Courts, and visitors are admitted to the public galleries. Courts generally sit in Term times: Weekdays, 10.30 a.m. to 4.30 p.m.    Station: Temple Cir.D.

■ **Royal Exchange,** Cornhill. 5A 74
Was opened by Queen Victoria in 1844, replacing two previous buildings on this site, burned down respectively in 1666 and 1838. The original Exchange of 1568 was modelled on the Antwerp Bourse.    *Station:* Bank Cen.N.

■ **Royal Festival Hall,** see South Banks Arts Centre.

■ **Royal Geographical Society,** Kensington Gore. 1F 89
Founded in 1830. Lowther Lodge was designed by Norman Shaw 1874. Important cartographic library, bibliographic archives and expedition relics. Open: Library and map room by appointment for research, fees apply. *Station:* Knightsbridge P

■ **\*Royal Hospital, Chelsea,** Royal Hospital Road, SW3. ✪
Was designed by Sir Christopher Wren and founded in 1682 by Charles II as a home for old soldiers. The 'Chelsea Pensioner' is a well-known figure in his scarlet (Summer) or dark blue (Winter) coat. The statue of Charles II in the Figure Court is by Grinling Gibbons. In part of the spacious gardens the Chelsea Flower Show is held annually by the Royal Horticultural Society.
Open: (a) Buildings and Museum open 10am. to 12pm. 2 to 4 p.m. Sun 2 to 4 p.m. Closed Bank Hols. (b) The grounds are open from 10 a.m. to dusk. Closed Christmas Day and Good Friday. Guide available by previous arrangement.    *Station:* Sloane Square Cir.D.

■ **Royal Mews,** see Buckingham Palace. ✪✪ ✪

■ **Royal Mint,** Tower Hill, 2E 87
It was here that our 'silver' and bronze coins were struck between 1811 and 1970, work since transferred to Llantrisant, South Wales. Prior to 1811 it was located in the Tower of London.    *Station:* Tower Hill Cir.D.

■ **Royal Naval College,** see Outer London. ✪

■ **Royal National Theatre,** see South Bank Arts Centre.

■ **Royal Opera House,** Bow Street,  5C 70
The home of the Royal Opera  and Royal Ballet companies, now fully modernised and restored with public areas, exhibition spaces and restaurants.
Open Mon to Sat. *Station:* Covent Garden P.

■ **St. Bartholomew's Hospital,** Smithfield. 3C 72
Popularly known as 'Bart's', this is the oldest hospital in London, having been founded in 1123 by Rahere, together with an Augustine Priory, in the reign of Henry I. The building contains portraits of famous physicians and surgeons of the hospital by Reynolds, Lawrence, etc., and

Hogarth's 'The Good Samaritan and 'Pool of Bethesda'. *Admission:* On application to the Clerk to the Governors. *Station:* St. Paul's Cen.

■ **St. James's Palace.** 4E 81 ✪
Built in 1532 by Henry VIII on the site of a leper hospital, this Palace was from time to time used as a Royal Residence after the Palace of Whitehall had been burned down in 1698. Charles II, James II, Mary II and George IV were born here. It was from here that Charles I took leave of his children before walking across St. James's Park to his execution, outside the Banqueting House in Whitehall.
The main gateway, the Tapestry and Armoury Rooms and the Chapel Royal are all that remain of the original building. *Admission:* To the Chapel for the Sunday morning service at 11:15 (Oct.-July).
*Stations:* Green Park J.P.V., St. James's Park Cir.D.

■ **St. James's Park.** 5F 81 ✪✪
These 93 acres were acquired by Henry VIII in 1531 to give him hunting near his Palace of Whitehall. It was under Charles I that the land was laid out by the French landscape gardener, Le Notre, to form one of the most charming of London's Royal Parks. A variety of water birds inhabit the lake, and these may be identified by labelled reproductions.
*Stations:* St. James's Park Cir.D., Charing Cross B.N

■ **St. Katharine's Dock,** St. Katharine-by-the-Tower. 2E 87
✪ Built 1827 to designs by Thomas Telford, these massive and secure warehouses were used to store valuable cargoes from all over the world. Historic structures have been restored and incorporated into a precinct of shopping arcades, restaurants and cobbled walks around a 240 moorings Yacht Haven.
*Station:* Tower Hill Cir.D.

■ **St. Martin-in-the-Fields,** St. Martin's Place 2B 82 ✪
This historic church rebuilt by James Gibbs 1721-61 is famous as a landmark in Trafalgar Square, also for its work with the homeless and public concerts. Visit the bookshop, gallery, craft market, restaurant and Brass Rubbing Centre (see below) *Station:* Charing Cross B.N.

■ **St. Paul's Cathedral,** St Paul's Churchyard. 5C 72 ✪✪✪
This is Sir Christopher Wren's masterpiece, built to replace the much larger Medieval Cathedral on the same site after its destruction in the Great Fire of 1666. The most prominent of London's buildings, this is an immense Renaissance structure, its exterior length being 515 ft, its width across transepts 250 ft., and the height from pavement to the top of the cross 365 ft. Together with many other chapels in St. Paul's there is the American

Chapel, which was dedicated in the presence of Queen Elizabeth II and the then Vice-President Nixon of the United States. Among the many famous people buried here are Christopher Wren, Nelson, Wellington, Jellicoe, Reynolds and Turner. 627 steps lead to the Whispering Gallery, Stone Gallery and to the Great Ball.
Services held daily. Open for visitors Mon. to Sat. 8.30 a.m. to 4 p.m. *Admission Charge for sightseers.* Visiting subject to restrictions during services and ceremonies. Open on Sundays for services only.
*Station:* St. Paul's Cen.

■ **Savoy Chapel,** Savoy Hill, Strand. 1D 83
The present Chapel was erected as part of a hospital founded under the will of Henry VII. It stands on the site of the old Palace of Savoy given to the Earl of Savoy by Henry III. Chaucer, it is believed, was married here during John of Gaunt's ownership. John of Gaunt had to flee, however when Wat Tyler's rebels destroyed the buildings in 1381. Open: Tues. to Fri. 11.30 a.m. to 3.30 p.m. Sun. service 11.00 a.m. Closed August and September.
Station: Embankment B.Cir.D.N.

■ **Science Museum,** Exhibition Road. 3F 89 ✪✪✪ ✪
Renowned and extremely popular collection of scientific, engineering and industrial exhibits both historic and modern. New displays include 'Making the Modern World', and exciting walk through some 2000 exhibits telling the story of innovation in science and technology, from the mid 18th c. to the present. Also the new Wellcome wing designed to show what is happening in science and technology today, features include an IMAX cinema and many hands-on exhibits like Launch Pad, Virtual Voyages, Pattern Pod and Digitopolis.
*Admission Charge.* Open: daily 10 a.m. to 6 p.m. Closed 24, 25, 26 December. *Station:* South Kensington Cir.D.P.

■ **Serpentine Gallery,** see Kensington Gardens.

■ **Shakespeare's Globe Theatre & Exhibition,** Bankside 3D 85 ✪✪ The reconstructed 1599 Globe Theatre, is the first thatched building in the centre of London since the Great Fire 1666. It is the centrepiece of the International Shakespeare Centre, which when complete will include a second indoor theatre to designs of 1617 by Inigo Jones.
*Admission Charge.* Open. Exhibition and tour daily May to Sept. 9 a.m. to 12.00 p.m. Oct. to April 10 am. to 5 pm. Tel: 020 7902 1500. Summer Season of plays Box Office 020 7401 9919. *Stations:* London Bridge J.N. Southwark J.

■ **Sherlock Holmes Museum,** 221b Baker Street. 1E 67
Modelled on the life and times of Sherlock Holmes and Dr Watson as portrayed by Sir Arthur Conan Doyle.

*Admission Charge.* Open 9.30 a.m. to 6 p.m. daily.
*Station:* Baker Street B.Cir.J.M.H.

■ **Silver Vaults,** 53 Chancery Lane. 3F 71
Underground strongrooms built in the 1880s as a Safe Depository. Now houses over 40 individual shops selling all types of silverware from contemporary to antique and Sheffield Plate.
*Station:* Chancery Lane Cen. (Closed Sun.)

■ **Sir John Soane's Museum,** Lincoln's Inn Fields. 3E 71 ✪
This house, was designed and built in 1812 by Sir John Soane, architect to the Bank of England, to contain his own museum, furniture, and library. Among the many unique exhibits are Egyptian, Greek and Roman antiquities, including the Sarcophagus of Seti 1; paintings by Canaletto, Watteau and Reynolds; and the finest collection of Hogarth's work, comprising the eight scenes of 'The Rake's Progress' and four of 'The Election'.
Open: Tuesday to Saturday, 10 a.m. to 5 p.m. Closed Bank Holidays. *Station:* Holborn: Cen.P.

■ **Smithfield.** 3C 72
Now chiefly known for its Meat Market. In the past, the 'smooth field' lying outside the city wall was variously used for jousting, for St. Bartholomew's Fair (held annually for centuries), and for many executions. Among those executed here were: William Wallace, beheaded in 1305 for supporting Robert Bruce's claim to the Scottish throne. Roman Catholic and Protestant Martyrs burnt at the stake—during the 16th and early 17th centuries—for their beliefs. Wat Tyler was struck dead in 1381 by the Lord Mayor, helping to bring the Peasants Revolt to an end.
*Stations:* Barbican Cir.M., Farringdon Cir.M.

■ **Somerset House,** Strand and Victoria Embankment 1D 83
✪ ✪ Like a huge palace around a central square, Somerset House was built 1776-86 in grand neo classical style by Sir William Chambers on the site of the 16th c. palace of the Duke of Somerset.
The building once housed the Navy Board, the Royal Academy and Royal Society, more recently the Inland Revenue and General Register Office.
The Courtyard with its fountain display, is now a public open space and events venue. The Courtauld Galleries occupy the Strand side and the Visitor Centre, Gilbert Collection, Hermitage Rooms, restaurants and 800ft. river front terrace make up the south side. *Admission charges.*
Open: 10 am to 6 pm. extended evenings for courtyard, river front terrace and restaurants.
*Stations:* Temple Cir.D. Charing Cross B.N.

■ **Sotheby's,** 34/5 New Bond Street. 1C 80

Founded in 1744 it is the oldest the largest firm of fine art auctioneers in existence. Sales of furniture, jewellery, silver, porcelain, pictures, books etc., held regularly except in August. Telephone 020 7493 8080 for details. *Station:* Bond Street Cen.J.

**South Bank Arts Centre.** 3E 83 ✪
One of Londons premier centres of cultural excellence on the site of the 1951 Festival of Britain. Visit the Royal Festival Hall and Royal National Theatre, both have a foyer open daily with cafe, bookshop, record shop and exhibitions. Here also are the National Film Theatre, BFI IMAX cinema and Hayward Gallery.
*Stations:* Embankment B.Cir.D.N. Waterloo B.J.N.

**Southwark Cathedral,** London Bridge. 3F 85 ✪✪
This fine Gothic edifice built upon a nunnery, was originally the church of an Augustinian Priory, founded under Henry I. St. Saviour's was inaugurated as a Cathedral under its present name in 1905. John Harvard, founder of Harvard University, U.S.A., was baptised here in 1607. Exactly 300 years later a chapel and window were erected in his memory by Harvard students. Fletcher, Massinger and Edmund Shakespeare—brother of William—are buried here. Open daily. *Station:* London Bridge J.N.

**Spencer House,** 27 St. James's Place. 4D 81 ✪
London's finest surviving 18th century Town House, built 1756-66 for the first Earl Spencer, an ancestor of the late Diana, Princess of Wales. *Admission Charge.* Open: Sundays only 10.30 a.m. to 4.45 p.m. (closed Aug. and Jan.). Access by guided tour only. *Station:* Green Park P.V.

**Spitalfields Market,** Commercial Street. 2D 75
This historic fruit and vegetable market is now the centre of a renewed Spitalfields area with its restaurants, shops and popular Sunday market. *Station:* Liverpool Street Cen.Cir.M

**Staple Inn,** Holborn. 3F 71
Dickens' description in 'Edwin Drood' remains true:
'Behind the most ancient part of Holborn, where certain gabled houses some centuries of age still stand ... is a little nook composed of two irregular quadrangles, called Staple Inn ... the turning into which out of the clashing street imparts to the relieved pedestrian the sensation of having put cotton in his ears, and velvet soles on his boots.' His Mr. Grewgious lived here, and so in real life did Dr. Johnson. Staple Inn was formerly one of the lesser Inns of Court. *Station:* Chancery Lane Cen. (closed Sundays).

**Stock Exchange,** The. Old Broad Street. 4A 74
Plays a key part in maintaining London's role as the leading international financial centre, its origins date back

to the 16th century when the first joint-stock company was formed.   *Station:* Bank Cen.N.

■ **Strand.** 2C 82
Universally known for its hotels, theatres and shops. From Trafalgar Square it extends eastwards for nearly a mile.
*Station:* Charing Cross B.N.

■ **Tate Britain,** Millbank. 5B 94 ✪✪✪
The national gallery of British art from 1500 to the present, from the Tudors to the Turner prize. This most comprehensive collection of British art in the world includes works by Blake, Constable, Epstein, Gainsborough, Hogarth, Lely, Kneller, Stubbs, the Pre Raphaelites, Spencer, Moore, Hockney and most notably the Turner bequest in its own wing, the Clore Gallery.
Also special exhibitions and retrospectives.
Open: 10 a.m. to 5.50 p.m.  daily.   Closed Christmas Eve and Day, Boxing Day.  *Station:* Pimlico V.

■ **Tate Modern,** Bankside. 3C 84 ✪✪✪
Housed in the transformed former Bankside Power Station is the Tate's collection of international modern art from 1900 to the present. It includes works by over 200 artists including Auerbach, Bacon, Braque, Cragg, Duchamp, Giacometti, Matisse, Picasso, Riley, Rothko, Warhol and many contemporary and controversial artists. Also special exhibitions and retrospectives.   Roof top restaurant with panoramic views over the City of London.  Open: 10 am. to 6 pm. daily, to 10 pm. Friday and Sat.  *Station:* Southwark J. Blackfriars Cir.D.

■ **Temple,** Fleet Street. 1F 83 ✪✪
A complex of quiet squares and courts, of quaint corners, these precincts preserve a remarkable feel of "old London".   Formerly the property of the Knights Templars— from 1184 to 1313—and then of the Knights of St. John of Jerusalem; it finally came into the possession of two Inns of Court— Inner Temple and Middle Temple.
Open: Middle Temple Hall 10 to 11.30 am., 2.30 to 4 p.m. Mon. to Fri. only. Temple Church 10 am. to 3 p.m. closed Mon. & Tues. All closed for public holidays.
*Station:* Temple Cir.D.

■ **Temple Bar,** Strand. 5F 71
Mentioned in records as far back as the 13th century, it was the western entrance gate to the City of London. The last Temple Bar erected by Wren in 1672, is now in Theobold's Park, Cheshunt Herts. The Griffin Monument opposite the Law Courts marks its original site.
*Station:* Temple Cir.D.

■ **Theatre Museum,** Russell Street, Covent Garden. 1C 82

✪ History of the Theatre from early Elizabethan times to the 1980's including Opera, Ballet, Music Hall, Pop and Pantomime. Also changing exhibitions of theatrical costume, prints, live theatre performances in studio theatre. *Admission Charge.* Open: 10 a.m. to 6 p.m. Tues to Sun. Closed Monday. *Station:* Covent Garden P

## ■ Tower Bridge Experience. Tower Bridge. 3D 87

✪✪✪ ✪ Discover the history of Tower Bridge, how it works, London in the 1890's, and enjoy the spectacular views from the 142 ft high walkways. Tower Bridge, one of the sights of London, was designed by Barry and Jones and completed in 1894, the two draw-bridges open to allow the passage of large ships, a bell rings before the bridge opens, halting all traffic.
*Admission Charge.* Open: 10 am. to 6.30 pm. Summer, 9.30 to 6 pm. winter.
*Station:* Tower Hill Cir.D.

## ■ Tower of London. 2D 87 ✪✪✪ ✪

Built in part by William the Conqueror in 1078 as a fortress to guard the river approach to London, this is the most perfect example of a medieval castle in England, the outer walls being added later.

The White Tower contains, besides its collection of firearms and execution relics, the finest early-Norman chapel in this country. The famous Crown Jewels are housed in Waterloo Block. Elsewhere is the Royal Fusiliers Museum. Wall Walk gives good views over the Tower and River.

Anne Boleyn, Katherine Howard, Lady Jane Grey, Margaret Countess of Salisbury, Jane Viscountess Rochford, Robert Devereux Earl of Essex, were executed on Tower Green.
*Admission Charge.* Open Summer: 9 a.m. to 5 p.m. Mon. to Sat. 10 a.m. to 5 p.m. Sun. Winter: 10 a.m. to 4 p.m. Sun & Sat. 9 a.m. to 4 p.m. Tues. to Sat. Closed Christmas Day and Boxing Day, New Year's Day.
*Station:* Tower Hill Cir.D.

## ■ Tower 42, Old Broad St. 4B 74

The former national Westminster Tower. 600 feet high, it incorporates three irregular shaped wings around a central core.*Station:* Liverpool Street C.D.H.

## ■ Trafalgar Square. 3A 82 ✪✪✪

Laid out as a war memorial and named after the victory of Trafalgar, the Square was completed in 1841. In the centre rises Nelson's Column, 170 ft. high overall, allowing Nelson a view of the sea. The lions at the base are by Landseer. Fountains and pigeons delight onlookers. Facing Whitehall is a 17th-century equestrian statue of Charles I, the Martyr

King.   *Station:* Charing Cross B.N.

■ **Trocadero, Piccadilly Circus. 2F 81** ✪
A loud, fast and brash entertainment complex, just the sort of thing children like !   Includes ROCK CIRCUS, an exhibition and audio-visual experience presenting the history of rock and pop music from the 1950's onwards, featuring both the stars and their music.
Attractions have individual admission charges.  Open daily 10 a.m. to 12 p.m. (1a.m. Fri. & Sat.).   *Station:* Picadilly Circus. B.P.

■ **University of London,** Russell Square. 2A 70
This Senate House, completed just before the Second World War, contains only the University Library, Institute of Education, and central administration. Many of the Schools and Institutes constituting the University, like University College, are located nearby; with others throughout the London area, and some beyond.
*Station:* Russell Square P.

■ **Victoria and Albert Museum,** Cromwell Road. 3A 90
✪✪✪  One of the worlds great museums of fine and applied art. It illustrates artistic achievement and craftsmanship throughout the centuries and is arranged into two groups (a) Primary Collections—of style, period or nationality. (b) Departmental Collections— sculpture, textiles, woodwork, etc.  Also special exhibitions of specific interest throughout the year. The museum incorporates the National Art Library.   *Admission Charge,* (free after 4.30 p.m.). Open 10 a.m. to 5.45 p.m. daily, also 6.60 to 8.30 pm. Wed. Closed Christmas Eve and Day, Boxing Day,
*Station:* South Kensington Cir.D.P.

■ **Victoria Embankment. 5C 82** ✪
This tree-lined thoroughfare was built in 1864-70 by Sir Joseph Bazalgette, it stretches from Westminster Bridge to Blackfriars Bridge about $1^1/4$ miles and is the shortest and a most enjoyable route from Westminster to the City with a variety of things to see. Starting from Westminster Bridge, there is a statue of Boadicea in her chariot by Thomas Thorneycroft 1902. The Royal Air Force Memorial. Beyond the railway bridge is part of the Victoria Embankment Gardens with the York Watergate in the west corner, the only surviving part of York House; the position of the gate indicates the former extent of the river.  Further along are Cleopatra's Needle, Somerset House, Temple and Temple Gardens.   *Stations:* Westminster Cir.D.J. Embankment B.Cir.D.N., Temple Cir.D., Blackfriars Cir.D.

■ **Victoria Tower Gardens,** Millbank. 2C 94
Views across the river to Lambeth Palace and Church, and downstream to County Hall and other buildings. Statues

include Emmeline Pankhurst, leader of the women's suffrage movement, and a bronze replica erected in 1915 of the Burghers of Calais by Rodin 1895.
*Station:* Westminster Cir.D.

■ **Vinopolis,** Bankside. 3E 85
Exhibition and multi-media tour of the worlds wines, wine tastings, shops, art gallery, restaurants. Admission charge. Open daily. *Station:* London Bridge J.N.

■ **Wallace Collection,** Hertford House, Manchester Square. 4F 67 ✪ The most representative collection in England of French 18th-century painting, sculpture, furniture and Sevres porcelain. It includes masterpieces by Rembrandt, Hals, Rubens, Reynolds, Gainsborough, Van Dyck, Velasquez and Titian; important collections of ceramics, goldsmiths' work, and European and Oriental arms and armour. Formed in the main by the third and fourth Marquesses of Hertford and the latter's son, Sir Richard Wallace.
Open: 10 a.m. to 5 p.m.; Sundays 12 to 5 p.m.
Closed Good Friday Christmas Eve, Christmas Day, Boxing Day, New Year's bay, May Day.
*Stations:* Bond Street Cen.J., Baker Street B.Cir.J.M.

■ **Wellcome Centre for Medical Science,** 183 Euston Road. 5F 61 Houses the Wellcome Library for the History and Understanding of Medicine, one of the largest medical libraries in the world, Open Mon. to Fri. and Sat. am. only. Also from late 2001 the Wellcome Gallery will show exhibitions exploring the culture of medicine through art, science and history.
*Station:* Euston Square Cir.M.H

■ **Wellington Arch,** Hyde Park Corner. 5A 80
Designed by Decimus Burton in 1828. Originally a statue of Wellington stood on top, this was replaced by the present group when the Arch was moved from the entrance to Hyde Park. The frieze is based on the Elgin Marbles to be seen in the British Museum.
*Station:* Hyde Park Corner P.

■ **Wellington Museum,** see Apsley House.

■ **Wesley's House, Chapel and Museum of Methodism**
City Road. 1A 74 John Wesley lived here for 12 years and died in this house in 1791. His own rooms and furniture are preserved, and the Museum contains a unique collection of his possessions. Wesley is buried in the graveyard behind the Chapel. *Admission Charge.* Open 10 a.m. to 4 p.m. Mon. to Sat. Closed Bank Hols. Chapel is also open for Sunday service (House and Museum open after Sunday service until 2 pm).
*Stations:* Old Street N., Moorgate Cir.M.N

■ **Westminster Abbey,** Parliament Square. 2B 94 ✪✪✪
One of the most interesting and historic religious buildings
in England; and architecturally one of the masterpieces of
the Middle Ages. Founded about 800 A.D. the present
edifice was planned and erected as a Royal Mausoleum
by Henry III in memory of Edward the Confessor, and until
George III most of the Kings of England were buried within
its precincts. Almost all have been crowned here; the only
two exceptions being Edward V, who was murdered
before he could be crowned, and the Duke of Windsor,
Edward VIII, who renounced the throne before his
coronation. The famous Coronation Chair is in Edward the
Confessor's Chapel.
Many famous men are buried in the Abbey; there is the
well-known Poets' Corner, and the grave of the Unknown
Warrior. Abbey Museum in the outstanding Norman
Undercroft shows the Abbey history and a remarkable
collection of Royal and Noble effigies and death masks.
Services held daily.
Open: *Admission Charge for sightseers*. Nave open daily
(Sundays between services only). The Royal Chapels,
Poets' Corner, Choir, and Statesmens' Aisle open Mon. to
Sat. only, Chapter House and Museum daily.
*Stations:* Westminster Cir.D.J., St. James's Park Cir.D.

■ **Westminster Cathedral,** Ashley Place. 3E 93 ✪✪
Opened in 1903, this is the foremost Roman Catholic
Church in England. The architect, John Francis Bentley,
who was influenced by the Christian Byzantine style of St
Sophia at Constantinople, died a year before the building
was completed. A lift serves the Campanile, which is 284
ft. high. In May 1982 Pope John Paul II celebrated the first
mass ever by a Pope on English soil.
Open 7 a.m. to 8 p.m. daily. Admission Charge for lift to
viewing gallery, open 9 am. to 5 pm. daily April to Nov. (On
Thurs. Fri. Sat. & Sun. only Dec. to March).
*Station:* Victoria Cir.D.V.

■ **Westminster Hall,** Parliament Square. 1B 94 ✪
The main surviving fragment of the old Palace of
Westminster destroyed by fire in 1834. Erected in 1097 by
William Rufus, it was rebuilt 1394-99 by Richard II who was
responsible for the magnificent oak roof spanning the
width of the Hall. Many famous State trials have taken
place here; among them those of Charles I, Sir Thomas
More, Guy Fawkes and Warren Hastings. Now used for
great functions and for 'Lying in State'.
For details of information for visitors, ring House of
Commons Information Office 020 7219 4272
*Station:* Westminster Cir.D.J.

■ **Whitechapel Art Gallery,** Whitechapel High Street, 4E 75

32

A charitable trust founded to organise temporary exhibitions of modern art.
*Admission Charge.* Open Tues. to Sun 11 a.m. to 5 p.m. Wed to 8 p.m. *Station:* Aldgate East D.M.H.

■ **Whitehall.** 4B 82 ✪✪✪
Part of the original palace of Whitehall, this famous thoroughfare extends from Trafalgar Square southwards to Parliament Square. At the entrance to the Horse Guards Parade, mounted guards are on sentry duty.
Downing Street, home of the Prime Minister, is a turning off Whitehall near the Cenotaph, the principal monument in the centre of the road. Many Government Departments are housed here.
*Stations:* Charing Cross B.N. Westminster Cir.D.J.

■ **Windsor Castle,** see Outer London. ✪✪✪

■ **Winston Churchill's Britain at War Experience,**
64/66 Tooley Street. 4B 86 ✪✪ Relive the drama of life during the Second World War; the Blitz comes alive with sound, smells and visual effects, experience how we lived through 'those darkest days'. Admission Charge. Open daily 10 a.m. to 4.30 p.m., until 5.30 p.m. Summer months. *Station:* London Bridge J.N.

■ **PLACES OF INTEREST, MUSEUMS and ART GALLERIES in OUTER LONDON**

*NOTE: These items are all outside the central area map. Many can be most easily visited by taking an appropriate coach tour, see Conducted Coach Tours.*

■ **Battle of Britain Museum,** also Bomber Command Museum. ✪ ✪ See Royal Air Force Museum.

■ **Box Hill,** Surrey
800 acres of National Trust woods and chalk downland famous for its magnificent views of the Downland countryside. Open: free access daily.

■ **Chartwell,** near Westerham, Kent ✪
For many years the country home of Sir Winston Churchill; the house is maintained as he left it, as is the studio where many of his paintings were executed. There are extensive gardens. Now a National Trust Property.
*Admission Charge.* Open: House, Garden and Studio 11 am. to 5.30 pm. daily (except closed Mon. and Tues.), April to Oct. House and Garden also open 11 am. to 4.30 pm. Sat. Sun. and Wed. in March and Nov.

■ **Chessington World of Adventures,** Leatherhead Road,

**Chessington, Surrey.** ✪ ✪    Theme Park and Fun Fair with over 100 attractions and rides; also zoo and skyway monorail. *Admission Charge:* Open: Mar. to Oct. only.
*Station:* Chessington South by train from Waterloo.

### ■ **Chiswick House,** Burlington Lane W4 ✪
A fine example of Palladian architecture built by Richard Boyle the Third Earl of Burlington in the late 1720's. The main front is composed of two double approach stairways flanking a classical portico at first floor level.
The interior with its series of connected rooms was designed by William Kent. There are marble fireplaces with support panels by Sebastian Ricci and paintings by Kneller, Lely and Guido Reni. The garden laid out by Kent was a forerunner to the English Landscape Park and contains some statues brought over from Hadrian's Villa at Tivoli near Rome. There are also statues of Palladio and Inigo Jones.
*Admission Charge.* Open: 10 a.m. to 6 p.m. summer months; to 4 p.m. winter months. Closed Mon. & Tues.
*Station:* Chiswick by train from Waterloo.

### ■ **Cutty Sark,** Greenwich, SE10 ✪✪✪ ✪
The last and most famous of the clipper sailing ships that raced to bring their tea cargoes to British ports. Adjacent is the diminutive Gipsy Moth 1V in which Sir Francis Chichester sailed round the world single-handed.
*Admission Charge:* Open: 10 am. to 6 pm. (5 pm. winter); Mon. to Sat. 12 pm. to 6 pm. (5 pm. winter); on Sun.
*Station:* Greenwich by train from Charing Cross or London Bridge. Or Docklands Light Railway to Cutty Sark Station. Or by riverboat from Westminster or Tower Piers.

### ■ **Docklands**
The Port of London was once one of the worlds largest ports occupying the banks of the River Thames from the Tower of London to Woolwich; during the 1960's and 70's industrial strife and new technologies bought about their decline and replacement by modern facilities at Tilbury.
Since then some eight and a half square miles of derelict or underused land and water has undergone a remarkable transformation. The Docklands Light Railway —automated and driverless— snakes through acres of modern developments, many attracting architectural awards. Among the features of interest are St. Katharine's Dock, Design Museum and Butlers Wharf, Hay's Galleria, Canary Wharf Financial Centre with Britains tallest tower block (800ft), New Billingsgate Fish Market, London City Airport, The Thames Barrier and the dockside ExCeL state-of-the-art international event venue.

### ■ **Dulwich Picture Gallery,** College Road, SE21 ✪

An outstanding collection of Flemish, Italian and Dutch Art. Paintings by Ruisdael, Van de Velde, Cuyp, Van Dyck, Rembrandt, Rubens, Claude, Raphael, Veronese, Murillo and Poussin, it also contains British 17th and 18th century portraiture, including Gainsborough and Reynolds.
*Admission Charge (free on Friday).* Open: Tues. to Fri. 10 am. to 5pm. Sat. and Sun. 11 am. to 5pm. Closed Mon. except Bank Holiday Mondays.
*Stations:* North Dulwich by train from London Bridge or West Dulwich from Victoria.

■ **Epping Forest,** Between Chingford and Epping
A relic of the ancient Royal hunting forest of Waltham. Now extending about 11 miles north/south, by 2-3 miles across, and managed by the City of London Corporation providing free public access at all times. Epping Forest Museum is in Queen Elizabeth's Hunting Lodge, Rangers Road, E14.
*Station:* Chingford by train from Liverpool Street.

■ **Estorick Collection of Modern Art,** 39a Canonbury Square, NI  A museum of modern Italian Art including the finest collection of Futurist Paintings outside Italy.
*Admission Charge.* Open Wed to Sat. 11am to 6pm. 12 to 5pm Sun.  *Station:* Highbury & Islington V.

■ **Fan Museum,** 12 Crooms Hill, Greenwich SE10
Is the world's first and only museum of fans; elegant displays in a fine early Georgian house with Orangery and landscape garden.
*Admission Charge.* Open: 11 am. to 5 pm. Tues. to Sat. From 12 pm. Sundays. Closed Mon.   *Station:* As for Cutty Sark.

■ **Freud Museum,** 20 Maresfield Gardens, Hampstead NW3
The study of the founder of psychoanalysis is kept exactly as it was in his lifetime, including his library, antiquities and the famous couch. *Admission Charge.* Open: 12 am. to 5 pm. Wed. to Sun. *Station:* Swiss Cottage J.

■ **Hampton Court Palace**, Hampton, Middlesex ✪✪✪
Built by Cardinal Wolsey in 1515, and at that time the largest and most magnificent palace in England, it aroused Henry VIII's envy and concern. Ten years later it was presented to him by the Cardinal, and from then until George II, remained a favourite Royal residence.
Set around the three principal courtyards, visitors can explore The Wolsey Rooms, Henry VIII's State Appartments and Chapel, the extensive Tudor Kitchens, William III's State and private apartments etc. The Renaissance Picture Gallery displays important works from the Royal Art Collection.  There are over 60 acres of grounds and gardens, which include the Privy Garden, the Orangery by Wren and the famous Maze.

*Admission Charge.* Open: 9.30 am. to 6 pm. Summer. 9.30 am. to 4.30 pm. Winter. (Opens at 10.15 am. on Mondays).
*Station:* Hampton Court by train from Waterloo Main Line Station. Or in summer, by boat from Westminster Pier.

■ **Hampstead Heath,** Hampstead, NW3
A great tract of undulating, informal parkland, among its many delights are Parliament Hill, with its kite flyers and superb views over London. See also Kenwood.
Open daily. Station: Hampstead N.

■ **Horniman Museum,** 100 London Road, SE23. ✪ ✪
Displays of arts and crafts, natural history, and a unique display of ethnic and western musical instruments. Also 'Living Waters', a conservation-minded aquarium experience. The gardens have one of the best views over London from the south, also animal enclosures.
Open: 10.30 am. to 5.50 pm. Mon. to Sat. 2 pm. to 5.50 pm Sun.   Station: Forest Hill by train from Charing Cross or London Bridge.

■ **Hogarth's House,** Hogarth Lane, W14.
The Queen Anne style country home of the artist Hogarth, now a museum of his drawings and engravings.
Open: 11 am. to 6 pm. Mon. to Sat. 2 pm. to 6 pm. Sun., April to Sept. (2 pm. to 4 pm. only Oct. to Mar.).
*Station:* Turnham Green D. P.

■ **Keats House,** Wentworth Place, Keats Grove, NW3.
Keats Regency home between 1818-20. Now a museum of personal relics.   Open: 10 a.m.-1 p.m., 2-6 p.m., Sat. 10 a.m.-1 p.m., 2-5 p.m Sunday 2-5 p.m. (Winter months not Mon. to Fri. a.m.).   *Station:* Hampstead N.

■ **Kenwood, Hampstead,** NW3 ✪✪
A classical style mansion set in 24 acres of parkland once owned by the first Earl of Mansfield. Designed by Robert Adam 1767-9 with additions by Saunders in 1795. Bequeathed to the Nation by the late Lord Iveagh in 1927, complete with his fine collection of paintings and furniture. Lakeside open air concerts held in the summer.
Open: daily 10 a.m. to 6 p.m. April to Sept.  Daily 10 a.m. to 4 p.m. Oct to March.  Closed Christmas Eve and Day. Park open 8 a.m. to dusk.
*Station:* Archway N. then Bus.

■ **Kew Bridge Steam Museum,** Green Dragon Lane, Brentford.   ✪   Steam pumping engines, related exhibitions and events. *Admission Charge.* Open: 11 am. to 5 pm. daily. 'In Steam' weekends and Bank Holidays.
*Station:* Kew Bridge by train from Waterloo.

■ **Kew Gardens,** Royal Botanic Gardens, Kew, Surrey.
✪✪✪ Beautifully situated by the Thames, contain over

25,000 different species and varieties of trees shrubs and plants from all over the world. There are two museums, a magnificent Palm House, Lily House, Rhododendron Walk etc. *Admission Charge.* Open: Daily from 9.30 am.
*Stations:* Kew Gardens D., or Kew Bridge by train from Waterloo. In summer, by boat from Westminster Pier.

■ **Legoland,** Windsor Park, Windsor , Berkshire. ✪
Theme park for children, built from and around the lego building block theme; rides, set display pieces and attractions in 150 acres of parkland.
*Admission Charge.* Open: Daily 10 am. to 6 pm. April to Sept. (to 8 pm. in Summer school Holidays). Weekends only in Oct. but daily autumn half term.
*Stations*: Windsor and Eton Central from Paddington, via Slough; or Windsor and Eton Riverside from Waterloo; then Legoland shuttle bus.

■ **London Butterfly House**, Syon House Gardens, London Road, Brentford. ✪✪ For a walk among exotic butterflies flying free within a tropical greenhouse. See also Syon.
*Admission Charge.* Open: daily 10 am. to 5 pm. (to 3.30 in winter). *Stations:* Gunnersbury D. then bus. Or Brentford by train from Waterloo.

■ **Museum of Fulham Palace,** Bishops Avenue, SW6
Illustrates the history of the Palace. The site, first acquired by Bishop Waldhere in 704, was the residence of the Bishops of London until 1973. *Admission Charge.*
Open: Mar. to Oct. 2 pm.— 5 pm. Wed. to Sun. Nov. to Feb. 1pm.—4 pm. Thur. to Sun. *Station:* Putney Bridge D.

■ **Museum of Richmond,** Old Town Hall, Whittaker Avenue, Richmond. Illustrates the long history of Richmond.
Open: 11 am. to 5 pm. Tues. to Sat. (Sundays 1pm. to 4 pm. May to Oct. only).
*Station:* Richmond D. or by train from Waterloo.

■ **National Maritime Museum,** Greenwich, SE10 ✪✪✪✪
The National Museum of our maritime history dealing with every aspect of ships and seafaring, in peace and war, from prehistory to today. Modern and stimulating exhibitions explore many historical event and characters, eg. Nelson, Trafalgar, Captain Cook, Battleships, Submarines. The Ship Hall has many interesting historic craft including the Royal Barge of 1689. See also Queen's House and Royal Observatory below.
*Admission Charge.* Open: 10 am. to 5 pm. daily.
*Station:* Greenwich by train from Charing Cross or London Bridge. Or Docklands Light Railway to Cutty Sark Station. Or by riverboat from Westminster or Tower Pier.

■ **Osterley Park House,** off Jersey Road, Isleworth.
A National Trust property administered by the Victoria and

Albert Museum. The house was begun in the 1560's as an Elizabethan Mansion for Sir Thomas Gresham, founder of the Royal Exchange. Later remodelled by both William Chambers and Robert Adam. Besides adding the portico, Adam designed the magnificent interiors and matching furniture. Outside are stables, parkland and the elevated M4 motorway !   *Admission Charge.* Open: Wed. Thurs. Fri. Sat. & Sun..11 am. to 5 pm.  Mar. to Oct.  Park daily. *Station:* Osterley P.

■ **Public Records Office,** Ruskin Avenue, Kew, Richmond, Surrey TW9 4DU.
Houses the National Archives accumulated since the Norman Conquest, including records created and acquired by the government. The Education and Visitor Centre mounts exhibitions featuring the nation's most famous documents and unique items of historical interest. Reading rooms are open to the public Mon. Wed. and Fri. 9.30am. to 5 pm. (last call for documents 4 pm.); Tues. 10 am. to 7 pm.;  Thus. 9 am. to 7 pm. (last call 4.30 pm.); Sat. 9.30 am. to 5 pm. (last call 3 pm.).  Closed Sundays, Bank Holidays and also Saturdays on Bank Holiday weekends.
*Stations:* Kew Gardens D. or Kew Bridge by train from Waterloo Main Line Station.
    Family Records are also held on microfiche at the Family Records Centre, 1 Myddelton Street, (Off Rosoman Street) EC1 4F 63 Open to the public Mon. to Sat. Closed Sun. and Bank Holidays.  *Station:* Angel N.

■ **Queen's House,** National Maritime Museum, Greenwich, SE10. ✪ Commissioned by James 1st, this Palace is a design by Inigo Jones, which, with his Banqueting House, Whitehall, marks the introduction of the classical ideals of Palladian architecture into England.  Exhibition displays form part and open as the National Maritime Museum.

■ **Rangers House,** Chesterfield Walk, Greenwich, SE10
This 18th. century house has a remarkable long gallery and collection of Elizabethan and Georgian portraits; once home of the fourth Earl of Chesterfield. *Admission Charge.* Open: 10. am to 6 pm. summer; to 5 pm. winter.
*Station:* see the National Maritime Museum.

■ **Richmond Park, Surrey.** ✪✪
An extensive Royal Park, first enclosed by Charles Ist. in 1637. This rolling landscape of forest trees and undergrowth, roamed by herds of deer, is big enough to get lost in. Isabella Plantation is a noted woodland garden. Open daily. *Stations*: Richmond D. or North Sheen or Richmond, by train from Waterloo.

■ **Royal Air Force Museum,** Aerodrome Road, NW9.

✪✪ ✪ Portrays the dramatic history of military aviation and aircraft from World War 1 onwards.
Battle of Britain Hall with its collection of fighter planes vividly displays the events and those involved in the battle for supremacy of the sky in 1940. Bomber Command Hall tells the story of the development of aerial bombing and displays many famous aircraft.
*Admission Charge.* Open: 10 a.m. to 6 p.m. daily. Closed Christmas Eve and Day, Boxing Day, Good Friday, New Year's Day, and May Day.
*Station:* Colindale N.

■ **Royal Naval College,** Greenwich, SE10 ✪
Stands on the site of the 15th. century Palace of Placentia, birthplace of Henry VIII and his daughters Mary and Elizabeth. Rebuilt by a succession of architects including Wren, the palace became Greenwich Hospital in 1705;
(the naval equivalent of the Royal Hospital for soldiers at Chelsea); and afterwards, in 1873, a college for the higher education of Naval Officers and now houses the University of Greenwich and (from 2001) Trinity College of Music.
The Visitor Centre, the magnificent Chapel of 1789 by James 'Athenian' Stuart and the unique Painted Hall by Sir James Thornhill are open: 10 am. to 5 pm. Mon. to Sat. and Bank Holidays, 12.30 to 5 pm. Sunday. Closed Christmas. *Admission Charge.*
*Station:* See National Maritime Museum.

■ **Royal Observatory Greenwich,** Greenwich Park, SE10
✪✪✪✪ Part of the National Maritime Museum housed in apartments built in 1675 by Wren for the first astronomer Royal. Deals with navigation, astronomy, time keeping and of course latitude and longitude. This is the home of Greenwich Mean Time and the Meridian Line, where you can stand with one foot in the east and one in the west ! and see the time-ball fall at 1 o'clock precisely.
Open as the National Maritime Museum.

■ **Saatchi Collection,** 98a Boundary Road, NW8
Changing exhibitions from the avant-garde Saatchi Collection of modern art. *Admission Charge,* (free Thurs).
Open: 12 pm. to 6 pm. Thurs. Fri. Sat. Sun.
*Station:* Swiss Cottage J.

■ **Syon House,** London Road, Brentford, Middlesex. ✪
The summer home of the Duke of Northumberland, Syon was originally a monastery built by Henry V in 1415. Much later a new house was built on the site incorporating parts of the monastery. The exterior remains largely unaltered, the interior was redesigned by Robert Adam in the 1760s with typical plasterwork, pillars and statues. There are many paintings, including portraits by Reynolds and

Gainsborough. Gardens laid out by Capability Brown.
See also the London Butterfly House.
*Admission Charge.* Open: HOUSE: Easter to End Sept.
Wed. to Sun. inclusive and Bank Hol. Mondays 11 a.m. to
5 p.m. also Sundays in October. GARDENS: Summer daily
10a.m. to 6p.m., Winter 10a.m. to dusk. Closed Christmas
Day and Boxing Day.
*Stations*: Gunnersbury D. then bus. Or Brentford by train
from Waterloo.

■ **Thames Barrier,** Barrier Approach, SE7
Built to save London from flooding, the Barrier consists of
huge movable steel gates pivoted between concrete piers;
hydraulic machinery can lift the gates from the riverbed in
30 minutes. On the south side an exhibition, audio-visual
presentation and viewing facilities are open for the public.
*Admission Charge.* Open: 10 am. to 5 pm. daily. 10.30am.
to 5.30 pm. weekends. *Station:* Charlton by train from
Charing Cross or London Bridge.

■ **Thorpe Park,** Staines Road, Chertsey, Surrey ✪
Theme Park and fun fair with over 70 attractions around a
lakeland setting; also working farm and craft shops.
*Admission Charge.* Open: daily summer months. *Station:*
Staines by train from Waterloo, then bus.

■ **William Morris Gallery,** Lloyd Park, Forest Road, E17
Devoted to the life and work of William Morris, his followers
and the Morris Company.
Open: 10 am. to 1 pm.; 2 pm. to 5 pm. Tues. to Sat. And
the first Sun. in each month. *Station:* Tottenham Hale V.

■ **Wimbledon Lawn Tennis Museum,** All England Tennis
Club, Church Road, SW19.
The history of tennis, displays of trophies and features on
tennis stars. *Admission Charge.* Open: 10 am. to 5 pm.
daily. *Stations:* Southfields D. Wimbledon Park D.

■ **Windsor Castle,** Windsor, Berkshire. ✪✪✪
A royal residence since William the Conqueror first built a
wood and earth castle here; this massive castle is now the
largest in England and dominates the town skyline. When
Her Majesty, Queen Elizabeth is here, the Royal Standard
flies from the Round Tower. The State Apartments, rebuilt
by Charles II, and richly furnished, contain many works of
art by the Old Masters from the Royal Art Collection.
St. George's Chapel, a superb example of Perpendicular
architecture, was begun for Edward IV as a private chapel
for Knights of the Garter. Windsor Great Park with its
famous Long Walk, and Virginia Water, once formed part
of the ancient Royal Forest of Windsor.
*Admission Charge:* Open: daily 10 am. to 5.30 pm. (last
entry 4 pm.), summer. Daily 10am. to 4 pm. (last entry 3

pm.), winter.

*Stations*: Windsor and Eton Central from Paddington, via Slough; or Windsor and Eton Riverside from Waterloo Main Line Stations.

## PAGEANTRY

### ◼ CEREMONY OF THE KEYS

Tower of London, continues after 700 years to be a 10 p.m. nightly event. The Chief Yeoman Warder—in scarlet coat, Tudor bonnet, and carrying a lantern—with foot Guard escort, locks up the several gates. On approach to the Bloody Tower archway, a sentry challenges:

*'Halt! Who comes there?'…'The Keys.'….'Whose Keys?'…..'Queen Elizabeth's Keys.'…….'Advance, Queen Elizabeth's Keys. All's well!'*

For admission write to: The Ceremony of the Keys, Waterloo Block, H.M. Tower of London, EC3N 4AB enclosing a stamped and addressed envelope.

### ◼ CHANGING OF THE GUARD ✪✪✪ ✪

BUCKINGHAM PALACE. Takes place at 11.30 on a variable timetable of alternate days, or daily when possible during the Summer months. For up-to-date information consult the London Tourist Board see pages 44 and 56 or the notice board at the Buckingham Palace gates.

The ceremony is carried out by one of the five regiments of Foot Guards, marching to the band, and resplendent in scarlet tunics and black bearskins (cancelled in very wet weather).

HORSE GUARDS Courtyard, Whitehall. Daily at 11 a.m. (Sundays, 10 a.m.) Ceremony by one of the two regiments of Household Cavalry either the Royal Horse Guard in blue tunics, or the Life Guards in scarlet. Traditional breastplates are worn by both regiments.

### ◼ LORD MAYOR'S SHOW.

A colourful annual procession (usually second Saturday November) when the newly-elected Lord Mayor drives in his gilded state coach, drawn by six horses to the Law Courts to take the oath.

### ◼ MAUNDY THURSDAY

The Queen distributes purses of money to as many poor people as the years of her age.

### ◼ OPENING OF THE ROYAL COURTS OF JUSTICE

The first Monday in October, all Her Majesty's Judges and members of the Bar—in State robes and full-bottomed wigs—attend a service in Westminster Abbey. Then, led by the Lord Chancellor, they walk in procession to the House of Lords; and after lunching there drive to the Law Courts.

The first Motion of the year, taken in his court by the Lord Chancellor, constitutes the opening of all the courts.

## ■ REMEMBRANCE SUNDAY
Annually, on the Sunday nearest November 11th, the Queen, the Prime Minister, Ministers, and members of the Opposition, take up their places by the Cenotaph, for the 11 a.m. two minutes silence Then the Queen leads the laying of wreaths in memory of those killed in battle since 1914.

## ■ STATE OPENING OF PARLIAMENT
After each General Election, and also annually normally at the end October or early November.

The Queen wearing her crown and robes of state, and escorted by Life Guards and Royal Horse Guards, is driven in her state coach along the Mall and Whitehall to the Houses of Parliament. There, in the House of Lords, she makes her speech from the throne, to both the Lords and Members of Parliament, who will have been summoned from the House of Commons.

## ■ TROOPING THE COLOUR ✪✪✪
Every June, on the Saturday nearest to the Queen's official birthday. This ceremony—dating from 1750—takes place on the Horse Guards Parade. The Queen, accompanied by Household Cavalry, and Guardsmen, travels there from Buckingham Palace and back again, to the strains of martial music.

---

## ■ BRASS RUBBING CENTRES

**St. Martin in the Fields,** St. Martin's Place. 2B 82
Open 10 a.m. to 6p.m. Mon to Sat. 12 to 6p.m. Sun.
**All Hallows by the Tower,** Byward Street. 2C 86
Open 11 a.m. to 4 p.m. Sun. 1 p.m. to 4 p.m. Summer season only.
**Westminster Abbey.** 2B 94 Open 9 a.m. to 5 pm. Mon. to Sat. Closed Sun.

---

## ■ FLOODLIT PLACES OF INTEREST

Admiralty Arch, Banqueting House, BBC Broadcasting House, County Hall, Dover House (Whitehall), Guildhall, Gwydyr House (Whitehall), Horse Guards, Houses of Parliament, Jewel Tower (near Westminster Abbey), Lloyds Building, Mansion House, Marble Arch, National Gallery, Old Admiralty, Old Bailey, Old Scotland Yard (Victoria Embankment), Old War Office (Whitehall), Royal Courts of Justice, Royal Hospital Chelsea, Royal Naval College

Greenwich, St. James's Park, St. Paul's Cathedral, Somerset House, South Bank Arts Centre, Tate Gallery, Tower of London, Trafalgar Square, Wellington Arch, Westminster Abbey and the following bridges— Albert, Chelsea, Lambeth, London, Vauxhall, Waterloo and Westminster.

## WALKS IN CENTRAL LONDON

Places in blue type appear in alphabetical order from page 2, together with description and admission times.
For COACH TOURS see Special Tourist Facilities.

One day: Starting at **Buckingham Palace** a walk along Birdcage Walk brings you to Parliament Square, with **Westminster Abbey**, the **Houses of Parliament** and **Big Ben**. Leaving Westminster Bridge on the right; walk up **Whitehall** past **Downing Street** and the **Horse Guards** to **Trafalgar Square**, where are **Nelson's Column** and the **National Gallery**. If your interests are historical and architectural take a bus along the **Strand** past the Law Courts to **Fleet Street** and **St. Paul's Cathedral**, and from there a bus to the **Monument**. A walk along Eastcheap and Great Tower Street brings you to the **Tower of London**.

If you prefer to see the West End shopping centre, take a bus from **Trafalgar Square** through **Piccadilly Circus** to **Regent Street**, walk north up to Oxford Circus, then turn left- west along **Oxford Street**, down **Bond Street**, and then left again at **Piccadilly**, which will bring you back to **Piccadilly Circus**, passing **Burlington Arcade**.

Two days: Take the underground to Tower Hill and nearby is the **Tower of London** with **Tower Bridge** beyond. Across the river are seen **H.M.S. Belfast** and the spires of Southwark Cathedral.
A walk along Lower Thames Street and past Old Billingsgate Fish Market brings you to the **Monument**, from which King William Street leads to the heart of the City, with the **Bank of England**, the **Mansion House** and the **Royal Exchange** among many other famous buildings. From here **St. Paul's Cathedral** is a short bus ride or walk. Almost any bus going down Ludgate Hill continues through what was once the newspaper centre of **Fleet Street** to the **Strand**. On the right are the **Royal Courts of Justice**, and in the middle of the road the island churches of St. Clement Danes and St. Mary-le-Strand.

The **Strand** opens into **Trafalgar Square**, with its fountains, Nelson's Column, **Admiralty Arch** and the **National Gallery**. Any bus down **Whitehall** passes the entrance to the **Horse Guards** where two mounted sentries are on guard. On the left is Inigo Jones's **Banqueting House,** from which Charles I was led to his execution. Government offices line **Whitehall,** and on the right is the famous **Downing Street.** The **Cenotaph** is slightly beyond and soon **Whitehall** opens out into Parliament Square.

Here, the **Houses of Parliament,** St. Margaret's Church and **Westminster Abbey** form an impressive group. Take a bus proceeding along Victoria Street—on the right is the **New Scotland Yard** building, on the left rises the Campanile of **Westminster Cathedral**—to Victoria Station, and walk along Buckingham Palace Road to **Buckingham Palace;** where the Royal Standard will be flying if Her Majesty the Queen is in residence. Walk along the tree-lined Mall and skirt the battlemented walls of **St. James's Palace,** Pall Mall, with its well-known clubs, is soon reached. Farther along Pall Mall is Waterloo Place, with the **Duke of York's Column** in the centre, and by turning left up **Regent Street** you come to **Piccadilly Circus.** A bus up **Regent Street** to Oxford Circus, and another along **Oxford Street** to Museum Street, brings you near to the **British Museum.** From here it is only a short distance to London University.

Three days: The same route should be followed, but more time devoted to the **Tower of London,** St. Paul's Cathedral, **The National Gallery** in Trafalgar Square, **Westminster Abbey** and the **British Museum.** Then take the Central Line underground from Tottenham Court Road to Queensway, and walk south along the Broad Walk through **Kensington Gardens.** On the right lies **Kensington Palace,** on the left the Round Pond. On reaching Kensington Road turn left to the **Albert Memorial,** the **Royal Albert Hall** and the museums: the **Science Museum,** the **Natural History Museum,** and the **Victoria and Albert Museum.** Close by is the Roman Catholic Brompton **Oratory** and the busy shopping centres of Brompton Road and Knightsbridge.

Four or more days: More time should be given to the places already mentioned that interest you most- but while in the **Strand, Lincoln's Inn** Fields and the **Temple** should be visited. It is a short walk to the **Victoria Embankment** to see the fine stretch of river with gardens, statues and monuments.

A short distance from **Oxford Street,** opposite Bond Street Station, is the **Wallace Collection** in Manchester Square. From Baker Street, nearby, buses go to **Regent's Park,** with its **London Zoo.**

## SPECIAL TOURIST FACILITIES

**TOURIST INFORMATION CENTRES**
**Britain Visitor Centre,** 1 Regent Street. 2F 81.Open: Mon.

to Fri. 9a.m. to 6.30 p.m. Sat. & Sun.10 a.m. to 4 p.m.
**City of London Information Centre** St. Pauls Churchyard.
5C 72. 020-7332 3456 Open: daily 9.30 a.m. to 5 p.m. April
to Sept. Winter months 9.30 a.m. to 5 p.m. Mon to Fri., to
12 noon Sat. Closed Sun.
**\*Greenwich Tourist Information Centre,** Pepys House, 2
King William Walk. SE10 020-8858 6376 Open: daily 10
a.m. to 5 p.m.
**\*Heathrow Terminals 1.2.3. Underground Concourse,**
Heathrow Airport.   Open Daily 8 a.m. to 6 p.m.
**\*Heathrow Terminal 3 Arrivals Concourse,** Heathrow
Airport.   Open Daily 6 a.m. to 11 p.m.
**Liverpool Street Underground Station,** 3B 74 Open:
Mon. to Fri. 8 a.m. to 6 p.m.  Sat. & Sun. 8.45 to 5.30 p.m.
**Southwark Tourist Information Centre,** 6 Tooley Street,
3A 86. Open: Mon. to Fri. 10 a.m. to  5 p.m. Sat & Sun. 11
a.m. to 5 p.m.
**Victoria Station Tourist Information Centre,** 3C 92.
Open: daily 8 a.m. to 7 p.m. Easter to Oct. reduced hours in
Winter season.
**Waterloo International Terminal,** Arrivals Hall, 5E 83.
Open daily 8.30 a.m. to 8.30 p.m.
**\*Windsor Central Station,** Thames Street, Windsor.
01753 852010  Open Mon. to Fri. 10 a.m. to 4 p.m. Sat. &
Sun. 10 a.m. to 5 p.m. (to 4 p.m. winter).

■ **LONDON TOURIST BOARD**
**Telephone Guide to Places of Interest and things to do**
09068 66 33 44
**Accommodation Advice** 09068 505 487
**Hotel Bookings Hotline** 020 7604 2890
Note 09068 calls cost 60p per minute plus any
hotel/payphone charges (as at August 2000).
Information is free to personal callers at Tourist Information
Centres, see above.

■ **TOURIST DISCOUNT CARDS**
**Go-See,** The London White Card Saver Pass to 16 major
museums. Available from Tourist Information Centres at
Victoria and Waterloo Stations, British Travel Centre,
London Transport Information Centres and participating
venues.
**London Pass,** combines admittance to over 40 visitor
attractions, a London Transport Travelcard and selected
boat trips. Available from the Britain Visitor Centre above.

■ **RIVER THAMES BOAT TRIPS ✪✪**
FROM WESTMINSTER PIER 1C 94
         CHARING CROSS PIER  3D 83
         WATERLOO PIER 5D 83
Regular trips to Tower of London, Greenwich and Thames
Barrier downstream: also services to Kew Gardens,

Richmond and Hampton Court upstream.

FROM TOWER PIER  3C 86
Regular trips to Greenwich and Thames Barrier downstream; and Westminster upstream; also across the river to HMS Belfast.

■ **CANAL TRIPS** ✪
Jason's Trip, Little Venice,  2D 65   For bookings, telephone 020 7286 3428.
*Jenny Wren Canal Trips, Camden Lock, Camden High Street, NW1. For bookings telephone 020 7485 6210.
London Waterbus Company, Little Venice, 2D 65 and
 * Camden Lock, Camden High Street, NW1
 020 7482 2550

■ **ROUND LONDON SIGHTSEEING TOURS** ✪✪
Circular tours run from the designated bus stops at many central locations, (Piccadilly Circus, Trafalgar Square etc.). They tour a variety of routes around the main tourist areas, and provide a hop-on, hop-off service for visiting the attractions on the route, spoken commentary, and usually open top buses.
London Pride Sightseeing  01708 631122
Original London Sightseeing Tour  020 8877 1722
Big Bus Company  020 8944 7810

■ **CONDUCTED COACH TOURS**  ✪
Tours are guide conducted in luxury coaches to some of the famous show places in and around London. All seats bookable. For information and to reserve seats apply to London Transport Travel Enquiry Offices, Victoria Coach Station or travel agents.

* Outside Central London area mapped.

■ **TRANSPORT INFORMATION**

■ Transport for London  24 hour information service
020 7222 1234.

■ **BUSES AND UNDERGROUND RAILWAY**
Information on services, route maps etc from Transport for London, 55 Broadway, Westminster, SW1 (and travel information centres, see below).
**24 hour travel information**  Tel: 020 7222 1234.
**Recorded travelcheck**  Tel: 020 7222 1200
For Central Area Underground Map see back cover.

■ **TRAVEL INFORMATION CENTRES**
King's Cross, Oxford Circus, Piccadilly Circus, St. James's Park, Heathrow Terminals 1.2.3 Underground Stations. Also Euston and Victoria Main Line Railway Stations.

■ **TRAVELCARDS**
Travelcards are on sale at Underground Stations, Transport for London Travel Information Centres, Main Line Railway Stations and London Tourist Board Information Centres.

Travelcards give access to London Buses and Underground trains, also the Docklands Light Railway and parts of the Rail system. Travelcards are good value, save time as well as the need to buy separate tickets for each journey. Travelcards can be bought for 1 day or 7 days (photograph required for 7 days). They cannot be used on coach tours.

■ **DOCKLANDS LIGHT RAILWAY**
Enquiries 020 7222 1234
From Bank Station 5F 73 or Tower Gateway Station 1E 87 to Lewisham (due open late 1999) via Canary Wharf, and Cutty Sark for Maritime Greenwich; or Beckton via Royal Docks; or Stratford via Bow.

■ **TAXIS**
Scale of charges is shown in each taxi-cab.

■ **COACHES**
Coaches travel from London to most Towns and Cities, seats must be booked in advance.
Victoria Coach Station, 164 Buckingham Palace Road.
Tel: 020 7730 3466. cc. bookings 020 7730 3499. 5B 92
National Express Coach Service Information 0990 808080

■ **GREEN LINE COACHES**
Connecting Central London with towns in the surrounding counties. Green Line Coach Station, Bulleid Way, Eccleston Bridge. 0870 608 7261. 4C 92

■ **MAIN LINE RAILWAY TERMINI**
Note: Through tickets for any station, irrespective of region, may be obtained from any station booking office. Seats and sleeping berths may be reserved in the same way.

■ NATIONAL RAIL ENQUIRIES 24 hours. daily
Tel. 0345 48 49 50.

Blackfriars 1B 84. Cannon Street 1F 85. Charing Cross 3C 82. Euston 3E 61. Fenchurch Street 1C 86. King's Cross 2B 62. Liverpool Street 3B 74. London Bridge 4A 86. Marylebone 1C 66. Paddington 4F 65. St. Pancras 2B 62. Victoria 4C 92. Waterloo 5F 83.

■ STATIONLINK A circular bus route linking the Main Railway Stations (not Charing Cross); especially for those who find it difficult to use other forms of travel, these buses offer a wheelchair ramp facility.

## ■ EUROSTAR
Through services direct to Paris and Brussels via the Channel Tunnel.
Waterloo International 5E 83. Information and Bookings Tel. 0990 186186 or 01233 617575.

## ■ AIRPORTS
**Gatwick,** Gatwick, West Sussex. 01293 535353
**Heathrow,** Hounslow, Middlesex. 0870 000 0123
**London City,** Silvertown, E16 020 7646 0000
**Luton,** Luton, Bedfordshire. 01582 405100
**Stansted,** Stansted, Essex. 0870 000 0303

## ■ AIRPORT LINKS
### ■ Gatwick-Central London
1. Gatwick Express, from Victoria Station.
2. Flightline Coach, from Victoria Coach Station.
### Heathrow-Central London
1. Heathrow Express, from Paddington Station.
2. Underground Train, Piccadilly Line to Terminals 123 or 4
3. Airbus 1, from Victoria Coach Station and limited stops including Knightsbridge, Brompton Road, Cromwell Road.
4. Airbus 2, from King's Cross and limited stops including Russell Square, Euston Station, Baker Street, Marble Arch, Lancaster Gate, Queensway, Holland Park Avenue.
### ■ London City-Cental London
Express Coach, from Liverpool Street Main Line Station.
### ■ Luton-Central London
1. Thameslink Rail service from King's Cross St. Pancras, Farringdon, City, or Blackfriars, to Luton Airport Parkway for connecting Shuttlebus service.
2. Greenline Coach 757 from Buckingham Palace Road, beside Victoria Station.
### ■ Stansted-Central London
1. Stansted Skytrain from Liverpool Street Station.
2. Express Coach service from Victoria Coach Station.

### ■ Heathrow-Gatwick-Stansted
**Jetlink** Express Coach, 2 hourly airport transfer service.

## ■ LOST PROPERTY OFFICES
**Buses, Underground** and on London Transport Executive Property: 200 Baker St., NW1. (No enquiries regarding lost property answered by telephone.)
**Other Lost Property:** Metropolitan Police Lost Property Office: 15 Penton St., N1,

**Main Line Railways:** At the Terminal Station of the Main Line concerned.

## PLACES OF WORSHIP

▪ **BAPTIST**
BLOOMSBURY CENTRAL CHURCH, Shaftesbury Avenue. 4B 70 *Station:* Tottenham Court Road
GOWER STREET MEMORIAL CHAPEL, Shaftesbury Avenue. 5B 70 *Station:* Tottenham Court Road
METROPOLITAN TABERNACLE, Elephant & Castle 4C 96 *Station:* Elephant & Castle
WESTMINSTER, Horseferry Road 3A 94 *Station:* St. James's Park

▪ **CHRISTIAN SCIENCE**
*FIRST CHURCH OF CHRIST, SCIENTIST, 8 Wrights Lane, W8 2B 88 *Station:* High Street Kensington
THIRD CHURCH OF CHRIST, SCIENTIST, Curzon Street. 3B 80 *Station:* Green Park
ELEVENTH CHURCH OF CHRIST, SCIENTIST, 1 Nutford Place. 4D 67 *Station:* Marble Arch

▪ **CHURCH OF ENGLAND**
ALL SAINTS, Margaret Street. 4D 69
*Station:* Oxford Circus
ALL SOULS, Langham Place. 3C 68
*Station:* Oxford Circus
CHAPEL ROYAL, St. James's Palace. 4E 81
*Station:* Green Park
CHRIST CHURCH, Commercial Street. 2D 75
*Station:* Aldgate East
ST. GEORGE (Hanover Square), St. George Street. 1C 80
*Station:* Oxford Circus
ST. GILES-IN-THE-FIELD, St. Giles High Street. 4A 70
*Station:* Tottenham Court Road
ST. JAMES'S, Piccadilly. 2E 81
*Station:* Piccadilly Circus
ST. MARGARET'S, Westminster. 1B 94
*Station:* Westminster
ST. MARTIN-IN-THE-FIELDS, St. Martin's Place. 2B 82
*Station:* Charing Cross
ST. MARYLEBONE, Marylebone Road. 1A 68
*Station:* Baker Street
ST. PAUL'S, Covent Garden. 1C 82
*Station:* Covent Garden
ST. PAUL'S CATHEDRAL, Ludgate Hill. 5C 72
*Station:* St Paul 's
SOUTHWARK CATHEDRAL, Cathedral Street. 3F 85
*Station:* London Bridge

WESTMINSTER ABBEY, Parliament Square. 2B 94
*Station:* Westminster

■ **CHURCH OF SCOTLAND**
CROWN COURT CHURCH, Russell Street. 5C 70
*Station:* Holborn
ST COLUMBA'S, Pont Street. 3D 91
*Stations:* Knightsbridge, Sloane Square

■ **DANISH CHURCH**
DANISH CHURCH, Regent's Park 2B 60
*Station:* Regent's Park

■ **DUTCH CHURCH**
DUTCH CHURCH, Austin Friars. 4A 74   *Station:* Bank

■ **FRENCH PROTESTANT**
EGLISE PROTESTANTE, FRANÇAISE DE LONDRES,
9 Soho Square. 4F 69
*Station:* Tottenham Court Road

■ **GREEK ORTHODOX**
ST. SOPHIA'S, Moscow Road. 1B 76   *Station:* Bayswater

■ **HINDU**
*SHRI SWAMINARAYAN MANDIR, 105/115 Brentfield
Road, NW10. *Station:* Neasden

■ **INDEPENDENT EVANGELICAL**
WESTMINSTER CHAPEL, Buckingham Gate. 2E 93
*Station:* St James's Park

■ **INTERDENOMINATIONAL**
AMERICAN CHURCH IN LONDON, 79 Tottenham Court
Road, 2E 69   *Station:* Goodge Street

■ **JEWISH**
CENTRAL SYNAGOGUE, Gt. Portland Street. 2C 68
*Station:* Gt. Portland Street
NEW WEST END SYNAGOGUE, 10 St. Petersburgh Place
2B 76   *Station:* Queensway
SPANISH AND PORTUGUESE SYNAGOGUE, Bevis
Marks 4C 74   *Station:* Aldgate
*SPANISH AND PORTUGUESE SYNAGOGUE, St Jame's
Gardens, W11 *Station:* Holland Park
WEST LONDON SYNAGOGUE (Reform), 34 Upper
Berkeley Street. 5D 67   *Station:* Marble Arch

■ **LUTHERAN**
ST. ANNE & ST. AGNES (LUTHERAN) CHURCH,
Gresham Street. 4D 73   *Station:* St. Paul's

■ **METHODIST**
CENTRAL HALL, Tothill Street, Westminster 1A 94
*Stations:* Westminster, St. James's Park
CHILTERN STREET WELSH METHODIST, Chiltern Street
2F 67   *Station:* Baker Street

(Last Sunday in month 6.30 pm only)
HINDE STREET CHURCH, Theyer Street. 4A 68
*Station:* Bond Street
WESLEY'S CHAPEL, City Road. 1A 74
*Stations:* Moorgate, Old Street.

■ **MOSLEM**
LONDON CENTRAL MOSQUE, Regent's Park. 4C 58
*Station:* Baker Street

■ **ROMAN CATHOLIC**
CHURCH OF THE IMMACULATE CONCEPTION, Farm
Street, Berkeley Square. 2B 80
*Stations:* Green Park, Bond Street
FRENCH CATHOLIC CHURCH OF NOTRE DAME DE
FRANCE, Leicester Place, off Leicester Square. 1A 82
*Station:* Leicester Square
ORATORY, THE Brompton Road. 3B 90
*Station:* South Kensington
OUR LADY OF THE ASSUMPTION AND ST. GREGORY,
Warwick Street. 1E 81    *Station:* Piccadilly Circus
*ST. BONIFACE GERMAN CATHOLIC CHURCH, Adler
Street, E1.    *Station:* Aldgate East
ST. GEORGE'S CATHEDRAL, St. George's Road. 2A 96
*Station:* Lambeth North
ST. JAMES'S, Spanish Place, Manchester Square. 3A 68
*Station:* Bond Street
ST. PATRICK CATHOLIC CHURCH. 21 Soho Square.
5A 70    *Station:* Tottenham Court Road
UKRANIAN CATHOLIC CATHEDRAL, Duke Street. 1A 80
*Station:* Bond Street
WESTMINSTER CATHEDRAL, Ashley Place. 3D 93
*Station:* Victoria

■ **RUSSIAN ORTHODOX CHURCH IN EXILE**
ALL SAINTS CATHEDRAL, Ennismore Gardens, SW7.
1B 90    *Station:* South Kensington

■ **SALVATION ARMY**
REGENT HALL, 275 Oxford Street. 5C 68
*Station:* Oxford Circus

■ **SOCIETY OF FRIENDS (QUAKERS)**
FRIENDS HOUSE Euston Road. 5F 61
*Station:* Euston Square
TOYNBEE HALL, 28 Commercial Street. 3E 75
*Station:* Aldgate East
WESTMINSTER MEETING HOUSE. 52 St. Martin's Lane.
1B 82    *Station:* Leceister Square

■ **SWEDISH**
SWEDISH CHURCH, 11 Harcourt Street. 3C 66
*Stations:* Edgware Road, Marylebone

■ **SWISS CHURCH**
EGLISE SUISSE DE LONDRES, 79 Endell Street. 4B 70
*Station:* Tottenham Court Road

■ **UNITARIAN**
ESSEX CHURCH, Palace Gardens Terrace. 3A 76
*Station:* Notting Hill Gate

■ **UNITED REFORMED**
CHRIST CHURCH AND UPTON CHAPEL, Westminster
Bridge Road. 2F 95     *Station:* Lambeth North
CITY TEMPLE, Holborn Viaduct. 3A 72
*Station:* St. Paul's
REGENT SQUARE, Regent Square. 4C 62
*Stations:* King's Cross, St. Pancras
ST. JOHN'S CHURCH, Allen Street, 2A 88
*Station:* High Street Kensington

■ **WELSH**
*WELSH PRESBYTERIAN CHURCH, 265 Willesden Lane,
NW2.  *Station:* Willesden Green

  * Outside Central London area mapped.

---

■ ░░░░░░░░░░░░░░░ **TICKETS** ░░░░░░░░░░░░░░░

Tickets should be bought from either the venue or a
reputable ticket agency.  Popular shows are often sold out
weeks or months ahead, it is however possible to queue
for 'returns'- returned tickets on the night of performance;
these are available only from the venue box office.  The
Half Price Ticket Booth can also offer tickets on the day of
performance.  Beware of ticket touts who may approach
you in such queues.

■ **Theatre, Concert, Events and Sports Ticket Agencies:**
Global: 020 7734 4555
First Call: 020 7720 0000
Half Price Ticket Booth, Leicester Square 2A 82 (open to
   Personal callers only).

■ **Hotel Booking Agencies:**
British Hotel Reservation Centre: 020 7730 5296
First Option Hotel Reservations: 020 7945 6030
London Tourist Board: 020 7824 8844
Nearest station shown in italics. §Membership required

---

■ ░░░░░░░░░░░░░ **WEST END CINEMAS** ░░░░░░░░░░░░░

ABC Panton Street. 2A 82 *Piccadilly Circus*
ABC Piccadilly Circus. 2E 81 *Piccadilly Circus*
ABC Shaftesbury Avenue. 5A 70 *Leicester Square*
ABC Swiss Centre. 1F 81 *Piccadilly Circus*

ABC Tottenham Court Road. 3F 69 *Tottenham Court Road*
BARBICAN 1 Silk Street. 2E 73 *Barbican, Moorgate*
*CHELSEA CINEMA 206 King's Road. SW3. *Sloane Sq*
CINE LUMIER Queensberry Place 4F 89 *South Kensington*
CURZON MAYFAIR Curzon Street. 4B 80 *Green Park*
CURZON MINEMA 45 Knightsbridge 5F 79 *Hyde Park Corner*
CURZON SOHO Shaftesbury Avenue. 5A 70
    *Piccadilly Circus*
§ICA Nash House, The Mall. 3A 82 *Charing Cross*
IMAX BFI Imax, Waterloo. 4F 83 *Waterloo*
METRO Rupert Street. 1F 81 *Piccadilly Circus*
MEZZANINE, see Odeon *Leicester Square*
§NATIONAL FILM THEATRE South Bank. 3E 83 *Waterloo*
*ODEON HAMMERSMITH Queen Caroline Street. W6
    *Hammersmith*
ODEON HAYMARKET, Haymarket 2F 81 *Piccadilly Circus*
*ODEON KENSINGTON HIGH STREET Kensington High
    Street. 2A 88 *High Street Kensington*
ODEON LEICESTER SQUARE 2A 82 *Leicester Square*
ODEON MARBLE ARCH Marble Arch. 5E 67 *Marble Arch*
ODEON WEST END Leicester Square. 2A 82
    *Leicester Square*
PRINCE CHARLES Leicester Square. 1A 82 *Leicester
    Square*
RENOIR Brunswick Square. 1C 70 *Russell Square*
SCREEN ON BAKER ST. Baker Street. 2E 67 *Baker
    Street.*
*SCREEN ON THE GREEN Islington Green, N1. *Angel*
UCI EMPIRE Leicester Square. 1A 82 *Leicester Square*
UCI PLAZA 1 & 2, Regent Street. 2F 81 *Piccadilly Circus*
UCI Whiteleys Centre, Queensway. 5C 64 *Queensway*
*UGC CHELSEA 279 Kings Road. SW3 *Sloane Square*
UGC HAYMARKET Haymarket. 2F 81 *Piccadilly Circus*
*UGC FULHAM ROAD SW10 *South Kensington*
UGC TROCADERO Coventry Street. 2F 81
    *Piccadilly Circus*
WARNER WEST END Leicester Square. 1A 82
    *Leicester Square*

*Outside Central London area mapped.

## WEST END THEATRES, OPERA & BALLET HOUSES

Nearest station shown in italics. §Membership required
ADELPHI Strand. 2C 82 *Charing Cross*
ALBERY St. Martins Lane. 1B 82 *Leicester Square*
ALDWYCH Aldwych. 1D 83 *Covent Garden*
AMBASSADORS West Street. 5B 70 *Leicester Square*
APOLLO Shaftesbury Avenue. 1F 81 *Piccadilly Circus*
APOLLO VICTORIA Wilton Road. 3D 93 *Victoria*

§ ARTS 6 Great Newport Street. 1B 82 *Leicester Square*
ASTORIA Charing Cross Rd. 4A 70 *Tottenham Court Rd.*
BARBICAN Silk Street. 2E 73 *Barbican, Moorgate*
BLOOMSBURY Gordon Street. 5F 61. *Euston Square*
BRITTEN OPERA THEATRE Royal College of Music,
   Prince Consort Road. 2F 89 *South Kensington*
CAMBRIDGE Earlham Street. 5B 70 *Leicester Square*
COCHRANE Southampton Row 4.1 71 *Holborn*
COCKPIT Gateforth Street. 1B 66 *Marylebone*
COLISEUM St. Martin's Lane. 2B 82 *Leicester Square*
COMEDY Panton Street. 2A 82 *Piccadilly Circus*
COTTESLOE See Royal National
CRITERION Piccadilly. 2F 81 *Piccadilly Circus*
DOMINION Tottenham Court Rd. 4A 70 *Tottenham Ct. Rd*
DONMAR WAREHOUSE see Warehouse
DRURY LANE Catherine Street. 5D 71 *Covent Garden*
DUCHESS Catherine Street. 1D 83 *Covent Garden*
DUKE OF YORK'S St. Martin's Lane. 2B 82
   *Leicester Square*
ENGLISH NATIONAL OPERA see Coliseum
FORTUNE Russell Street. 5C 70 *Covent Garden*
GARRICK Charing Cross Road. 2B 82 *Leicester Square*
GIELGUD Shaftesbury Avenue. 1F 81 *Piccadilly Circus*
GLOBE See Shakespeare's Globe
HAYMARKET Haymarket. 2A 82 *Piccadilly Circus*
HER MAJESTY'S Haymarket. 3F 81 *Piccadilly Circus*
§ ICA Carlton House Terrace 3A 82 *Charing Cross*
*LABATT'S APOLLO HAMMERSMITH Queen Caroline
   Street, W6. *Hammersmith*
LYCEUM Wellington Street. ID 83 *Charing Cross*
LYRIC Shaftesbury Avenue. 1F 81 *Piccadilly Circus*
*LYRIC HAMMERSMITH King Street. W6 *Hammersmith*
LYTTELTON See Royal National
NATIONAL Upper Ground, South Bank. 3E 83 *Waterloo*
NEW LONDON Drury Lane. 4C 71 *Covent Garden*
OLD VIC Waterloo Road. 5A 84 *Waterloo*
OLIVIER See Royal National
OPEN AIR Regent's Park. 4F 59 *Baker Street.*
PALACE Shaftesbury Avenue. 5A 70 *Leicester Square*
PALLADIUM Argyll Street. 5D 69 *Oxford Circus*
PEACOCK Portugal Street. 5D 71 *Holborn*
PHOENIX Charing Cross Road. 5A 70 *Tottenham Court Rd.*
PICCADILLY Denman Street. 1E 81 *Piccadilly Circus*
§ PLAYERS' Villiers Street. 3C 82 *Embankment*
PLAYHOUSE Northumberland Avenue, 3C 82
   *Charing Cross*
PRINCE EDWARD Old Compton Street 5F 69
   *Leicester Square*
PRINCE OF WALES Coventry Street. 2F 81
   *Piccadilly Circus*

QUEENS Shaftesbury Avenue. 1F 81 *Piccadilly Circus*
§RAYMOND REVUEBAR Brewer Street. 1F 81
   *Piccadilly Circus*
ROYAL COURT Sloane Square. 5F 91
ROYAL NATIONAL THEATRE Upper Ground, South
   Bank, 3E 83 *Waterloo*
ROYAL OPERA HOUSE Covent Garden. 5C 70 *Covent
   Garden*
ROYAL SHAKESPEARE COMPANY See Barbican
*SADLER'S WELLS Rosebery Avenue. EC1 *Angel*
ST. MARTIN'S West Street. 1B 82 *Leicester Square*
SAVOY Strand. 2D 83 *Embankment*
SHAFTESBURY Shaftesbury Avenue. 4B 70
   *Tottenham Court Road*
SHAKESPEARE'S GLOBE Bankside. 3D 85
   *London Bridge*
SOHO THEATRE & WRITERS CENTRE Dean St. 5F 69
STRAND Aldwych. 1D 83 *Covent Garden*
THEATRE ROYAL DRURY LANE see Drury Lane
THEATRE ROYAL HAYMARKET see Haymarket
*THEATRE ROYAL STRATFORD EAST Gerry Raffles
   Square. E15 *Stratford*
VAUDEVILLE Strand. 2C 82 *Embankment*
VICTORIA PALACE Victoria Street. 3C 92 *Victoria*
WAREHOUSE Earlham Street. 5B 70 *Leicester Square*
WESTMINSTER Palace Street. 2D 93 *Victoria*
WHITEHALL Whitehall. 3B 82 *Charing Cross*
WYNDHAM'S Charing Cross Road.1B 82 *Leicester Square*
YOUNG VIC The Cut. 5A 84 *Waterloo*
* Outside Central London area mapped.

## CONCERT HALLS

BARBICAN HALL Silk Street. 2E 73 *Barbican, Moorgate*
CENTRAL HALL Tothill Street. 1A 94 *St. James's Park*
CONWAY HALL Red Lion Square. 2D 71 *Holborn*
GUILDHALL SCHOOL OF MUSIC & DRAMA Barbican.
   2E 73 *Barbican, Moorgate*
LOGAN HALL Institute of Education, 20 Bedford Way.
   1A 70 *Russell Square*
PURCELL ROOM South Bank. 3E 83 *Waterloo*
QUEEN ELIZABETH HALL South Bank. 3E 83 *Waterloo*
ROYAL ALBERT HALL Kensington Gore. 1F 89
   *South Kensington*
ROYAL COLLEGE OF MUSIC Prince Consort Road.
   2F 89 *South Kensington*
ROYAL FESTIVAL HALL Belvedere Road, South Bank.
   4E 83 *Waterloo*
ST. JOHN'S Smith Square. 3B 94 *Westminster*
*SADLER'S WELLS Rosebery Avenue. EC1 *Angel*

*WEMBLEY ARENA  Empire Way, Wembley.
  *Wembley Park*
WIGMORE HALL 36 Wigmore Street. 4B 68  *Bond Street.*
  *Oxford Circus*

\* Outside Central London area mapped.

## GOVERNMENT OFFICES

Admiralty (Old Building) –
  4A 82
Commonwealth Office –
  5B 82
Department of the
  Environment – 2D 93
Foreign Office – 5B 82
Home Office – 1F 93–
Houses of Parliament –
  1C 94

Land Registry – 4E 71
Ministry of Defence – 4C 82
Northern Ireland Office –
  1B 94
Passport Office – 2E 93
  (4C 92  after April 2001)
Patent Office – 3E 71
Scottish Office – 5B 82
Treasury – 5B 82
Welsh Office – 5B 82

## SELECTED SHOPS

Army and Navy Stores –
  3E 93
Austin Reed – 2D 81
Debenhams – 5B 68
D. H. Evans – 5B 68
Dickins and Jones – 5D 69
Fenwick – 1C 80
Fortnum and Mason – 3E 81
Foyle's – 5A 70
Geographers' A-Z Map
  Company – 2F 71
Hamleys – 1D 81
Harrods – 2D 91
Harvey Nichols – 1E 91
Heals – 2F 69

John Lewis – 5C 68
Liberty – 5D 69
London Pavilion – 2F 81
Mappin and Webb – 1D 81
Marks and Spencer
  (Marble Arch) – 5F 67
Marks and Spencer
  (Oxford Circus) – 5D 69
Peter Jones – 5E 91
Peter Robinson – 4D 69
Selfridges – 5A 68
Thomas Neal's – 5B 70
Trocadero Centre – 1F 81
West London Silver Vaults –
  3F 71
Whiteleys Centre – 5B 64

## AUCTIONEERS

Bonham and Sons – 2C 90
Christies – 3E 81 & 5F 89

Phillips – 5B 68
Sotheby's – 1C 80

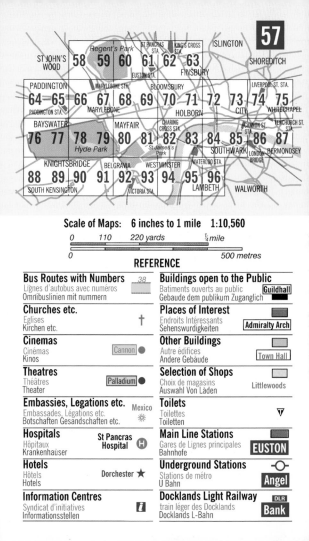

# 57

| ST JOHN'S WOOD | **58** | Regent's Park **59** | **60** | **61** | ST PANCRAS STA. **62** | KING'S CROSS STA. **63** | ISLINGTON | SHOREDITCH |

EUSTON STA.

FINSBURY

| PADDINGTON | MARYLEBONE STA. | | BLOOMSBURY | | | | LIVERPOOL ST. STA. |
| **64–65** | **66** | **67** | **68** | **69** | **70** | **71** | **72** | **73** | **74** | **75** |

PADDINGTON STA.    MARYLEBONE    HOLBORN    CITY    WHITECHAPEL

| BAYSWATER | | MAYFAIR | | CHARING CROSS STA. | | | | CANNON ST. STA. | FENCHURCH ST. STA. |
| **76** | **77** | **78** | **79** | **80** | **81** | **82** | **83** | **84** | **85** | **86** | **87** |

Hyde Park    St James's Park    SOUTHWARK    LONDON BRIDGE    BERMONDSEY

| KNIGHTSBRIDGE | | BELGRAVIA | | WESTMINSTER | | WATERLOO STA. | |
| **88** | **89** | **90** | **91** | **92** | **93** | **94** | **95** | **96** |

SOUTH KENSINGTON    VICTORIA STA.    LAMBETH    WALWORTH

## Scale of Maps: 6 inches to 1 mile 1:10,560

0    110    220 yards    ¼ mile

0    500 metres

## REFERENCE

**Bus Routes with Numbers** _38_
Lignes d'autobus avec numéros
Omnibuslinien mit nummern

**Churches etc.** †
Eglises
Kirchen etc.

**Cinemas** Cannon ●
Cinémas
Kinos

**Theatres** Palladium ●
Théâtres
Theater

**Embassies, Legations etc.** Mexico ✳
Embassades, Légations etc.
Botschaften Gesandschaften etc.

**Hospitals** St Pancras Hospital Ⓗ
Hôpitaux
Krankenhäuser

**Hotels** Dorchester ★
Hôtels
Hotels

**Information Centres** 𝒊
Syndicat d'initiatives
Informationsstellen

**Buildings open to the Public** Guildhall
Batiments ouverts au public
Gebäude dem publikum Zugänglich

**Places of Interest** Admiralty Arch
Endroits Intéressants
Sehenswurdigkeiten

**Other Buildings** Town Hall
Autre édifices
Andere Gebäude

**Selection of Shops** Littlewoods
Choix de magasins
Auswahl Von Läden

**Toilets** ▽
Toilettes
Toiletten

**Main Line Stations** EUSTON
Gares de Lignes principales
Bahnhofe

**Underground Stations** –O–
Stations de métro Angel
U Bahn

**Docklands Light Railway** DLR Bank
train léger des Docklands
Docklands L-Bahn

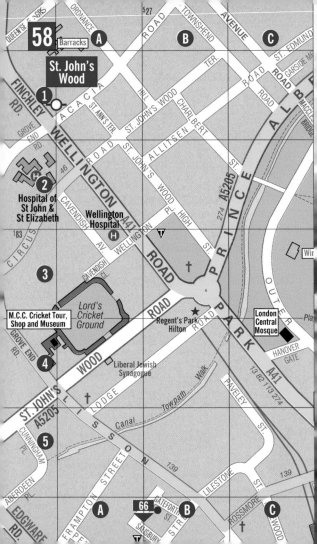

**58**

St. John's Wood

Barracks

Hospital of St John & St Elizabeth

Wellington Hospital

M.C.C. Cricket Tour, Shop and Museum

Lord's Cricket Ground

Regent's Park Hilton

Liberal Jewish Synagogue

London Central Mosque

HANOVER GATE

527

QUEEN'S GROVE
ORDNANCE
TOWNSHEND
AVENUE
ST. EDMUND
ROAD
GARSIDE
FINCHLEY RD.
WELLINGTON
ACACIA ROAD
ST. ANN'S TER.
ST. JOHN'S
HILL
CHARLBERT
TER.
MACCLE
BRIDGE
GROVE END RD.
CAVENDISH
46
ROAD
ALLITSEN
ROAD
ST.
PRINCE ALBERT
A41
WOOD
PL.
HIGH
ST.
A5205
274
CIRCUS
183
AV.
WELLINGTON
ROAD
PARK
OUTER
Win
CAVENDISH CL.
ROAD
PARK
ROAD
A41
GROVE END RD.
WOOD
ROAD
LODGE
Towpath
Walk
PAVELEY
ST.
13 82 113 274
ST. JOHN'S
A5205
LISSON
Canal
ST.
139
CUNNINGHAM PL.
STREET
ROSSMORE
WOOD
ABERDEEN PL.
EDGWARE RD.
FRAMPTON
SALISBURY
LILESTONE
ST.
139
66
GATEFORTH ST.

A B C

TER.
WELLS
RST
**D**

ROAD
274 528

Regent's Canal CIRCLE

**London Zoo**

**1**

Grand Union Canal

OUTER

# R E G E N T ' S
## P A R K

**2**

Refreshments

**60** ments
193

**3**

St. John's
Lodge

ield House

ground

INNER
● Open Air
CIRCLE
CHE

Children's
Boating
Pond

**Boating Lake**

Queen Mary's
Gardens

**4**

Ryl. Coll. of
bstetricians &
ynaecologists

London
Business
School

Bandstand

**5**

189 ROAD
RD
TAUNTON PL.
GLOUCESTER
BALCOMBE
BOSTON PL.
PL.
**D**

Americana

Bandstand

Regent's
College

Clarence Gate

YORK BRIDGE

Sherloc
Holmes
Museum
**E** ALLSOP

OUTER
**67** **F**
528

**Madame**

Royal Aca
of Mu

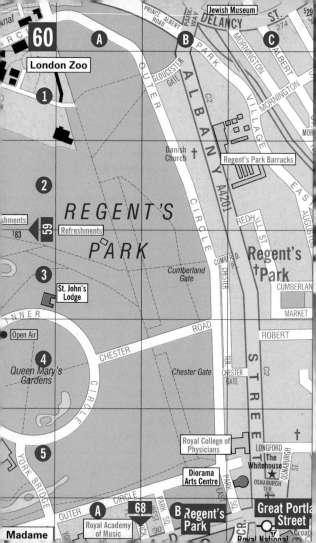

**A**

**B**

**C**

**Jewish Museum**

PRINCE ALBERT ROAD

PARK WAY

DELANCY ST.

529

274

MORNINGTON

ALBERT

**London Zoo**

**1**

GLOUCESTER GATE

OUTER

A L B A N Y

PARK

VILLAGE

MORNINGTON

MOR

C2

Danish Church †

**Regent's Park Barracks**

A4201

**2**

*REGENT'S*

CIRCLE

REDHILL ST.

EAST

AUGUST

shments

**59**
183

**Refreshments**

*PARK*

**3**

**St. John's Lodge**

Cumberland Gate

CUMBERLD.

CHESTER

**Regent's †Park**

CUMBERLAN

MARKET

INNER

**Open Air**

**4**

*Queen Mary's Gardens*

CHESTER

ROAD

Chester Gate

TER.

CHESTER GATE

C2

ROBERT

S
T
R
E
E
T

**5**

CIRCLE

YORK BRIDGE

**Royal College of Physicians**

LONGFORD

**The Whitehouse** ★

OSNABURGH

**Diorama Arts Centre**

PARK EAST

OSNABURGH TER.

†

**A**

OUTER

CIRCLE

YOR

**68**

**Royal Academy of Music**

ICK

PARK SQ.

**B**

PARK SQ. EAST

**Regent's Park**

CR

**Great Portland Street**

◯

Croft

**Madame**

**Royal National**

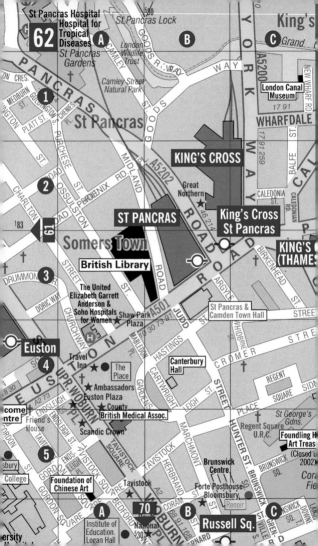

Cross

**D** Canal

**E** CHARLOTTE T.

**F** COPENHAGEN ST.

**63**

CARNEGIE ST.

17.91 269

259

WYNFORD RD.

CALSHOT ST.

RODNEY ST.

MURIEL ST.

CHARLOTTE ST.

BARNSBURY RD.

CLOUDESLEY RD.

LIVERPOOL

Canal Tunnel

RISINGHILL ST.

PENTON ST.

CHAPEL ST.

TOLPUDDLE ST.

MARKET ST.

**1**

**Pentonville**

COLLIER STREET

CALSHOT STREET

RODNEY STREET

STREET

DONEGAL ST.

WHITE ST.

STREET

BARON ST.

LION ST.

30 73 214

Crafts Council & Gallery ■

NORTHDOWN ST.

A5203

RD.

**PENTONVILLE** A501

30 73 214

WESTON RISE

ROAD

CLAREMONT SQUARE

**2** The Angel Centre

**KING'S**

PENTON RISE

AMWELL ST.

MYDDELTON '83

**ROSS LINK)**

BRITANNIA ST.

Royal National Throat, Nose & Ear Hosp. Ⓗ

Thistle King's Cross ★

INGLEBERT SQUARE

†

SWINTON ST.

CROSS

PERCY CIRCUS

GT. PERCY ST.

PERCY ST.

LLOYD ST.

RIVER ST.

**3**

**GRAY'S**

ACTON ST.

Clerkenwell Magistrates Court

LLOYD S'QUARE

STREET

FREDERICK ST.

CUBITT ST.

WHARTON ST.

LLOYD BAKER ST.

HARDWICK S.

ROSOMAN ST.

SOUTH ST.

London Ryan ★

MARGERY ST.

**4** Finsbury Town Hall

A5200

Kingsway Coll. ■

INN

63

ROAD

PAKENHAM ST.

**Clerkenwell**

TYSOE ST.

**5** London Metropolitan Archives

Ⓗ

The Eastman Dental Hospital & Institute

Holiday Inn

FARRINGDON

AV.

EXMOUTH MKT.

BOWLING GRN.

 spital res

Mecklenburgh Sq.

CALTHORPE ST.

PHOENIX PL.

Post Office Mount Pleasant

ROSEBERY

ROAD

FARRINGDON

Mecklenburgh Sq. Gdns.

DOUGHTY ST.

GOUGH ST.

BOWLING GRN. LA.

MECKLENBURGH PL.

BURGH ST.

**D**

MILLMAN

DOUGHTY M.

**E** Dickens House

**71**

**F**

WARNER ST.

RAY ST.

531

341

ROGER

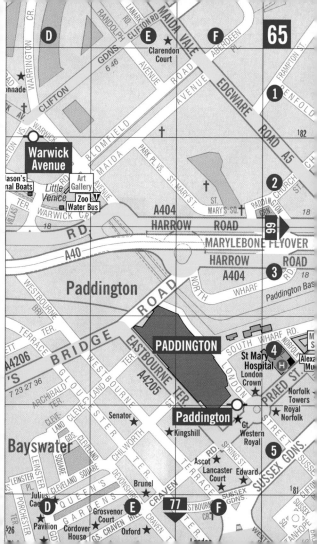

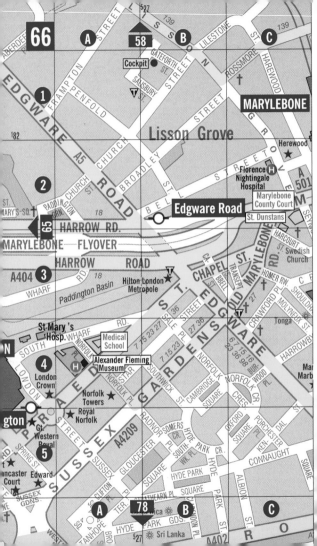

**A**  **B**  **C**

The Clerk's Well

Marx Memorial Library

55 243 505

St Bartholomew's Medical College

Charterhouse

WARNER ST.
19 38 341

**1**

CLERKENWELL

St John's Gate

Charterhouse

London Leather Centre

**2**

Farringdon

The Rookery ★

COWCROSS

Barbican

63 243

St Ethelreda's
45 46 243

Central Market (Smithfield)

St Bartholomew the

**71**

GREVILLE

HOLBORN

A40

HOLBORN

153

**3**

Central Market (Smithfield)

WEST  SMITHFIELD

St Bartholomew the Less

8 25 242
501 527  St. Sepulchre

HOLBORN CIR.

City Temple

VIADUCT  NEWGATE

St Bartholomew's Hospital

56

**4**

Old Public Record Office

Dr. Johnson's House

CITY (THAMESLINK)

45 46

Ye Old Cheshire Cheese

STONE CUTTER

45 63

St Pa

Central Criminal Court (Old Bailey)

St Pa

**5**

4 1115
23 26 76

FLEET

St. Bride's

PILGRIM

St Paul's Cath

Prince Henry's Room

Crypt Museum

LUDGATE HILL

Stationers Hall
17 23 26

Bar

Library

LUDGATE CIR.

45 63
172

Apothecaries Hall

CARTER

Inner Temple

Hall

St. Andrew

College of Arms

The Temple

**A**  **84**  **B**  Blackfriars  **C**  QUEE

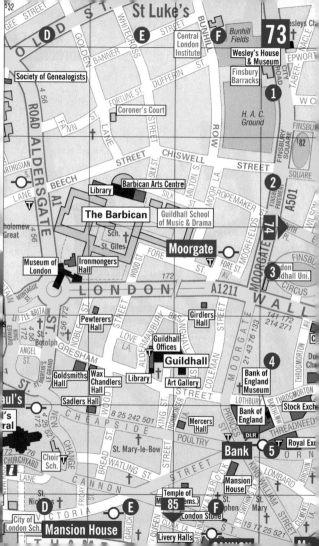

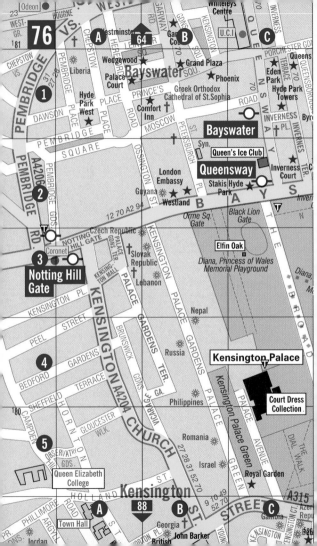

LEINSTER
SQUARE
CLEVELAND SQUARE
CHILWORTH
GLOUCESTER
TERRACE
Ascot ★ Road
Lancaster ★
Edward ★

**D** **E** 65 **F** **77**

LEINSTER
PL
Julius ★
Caesar

QUEEN'S GARDENS
DEVONSHIRE
CRAVEN
TER
WESTBOURNE
TER
Westbourne
CR
Sussex
GDNS.

SUSSEX
CLIFTON
SQUARE
STANHOPE
BROOK
ST.

PORCHESTER
Pavilion ★
Blakemore ★
Henry ★
VIII
n ★
York ★
Queen's ★
Park
ntral ★
ark
**W**
Thistle ★
Kensington
Gardens
ess Ter
rate

Grosvenor
Court ★
Cordover ★
House
London ★
House
Commodore ★
Hyde Park ★
Ryan

CRAVEN HILL GDNS.
CRAVEN HILL
Oxford ★
Mornington ★
Lancaster

CRAVEN TER
London ★
Elizabeth
Averard ★

WESTBOURNE
STREET

**1**

Leinster ★
House
Thistle ★
Hyde Park

LEINSTER TER
L A N C A S T E R
GATE
Plaza on ★
Hyde Park

LANCASTER
TERRACE

**Lancaster Gate**

Marlborough
Gate

Lancaster
Gate
Porchester
Ter. Gate

W A L K
WALK
Lancaster
Gate

The
Fountains

**2**

BUCK

Speke's
Monument

LANCASTER

WALK

THE LONG WATER

78

Peter Pan Statue

BUDGE'S

**3**

Princess of Wales
morial
Walk

K E N S I N G T O N

Physical Energy ●

**4**

ROUND POND

Serpentine Gallery

**5**

Bandstand

G A R D E N S

WALK

WALK

WALK

FLOWER

Albert Memorial

89

Alexandra
Gate

SOUTH

**D**
aijan
olic

**E**
Kensington Palace ★
Palace
Gate

THE
Queen's
Gate

89

**F**

Royal
College

K E N S I N G T O N RD

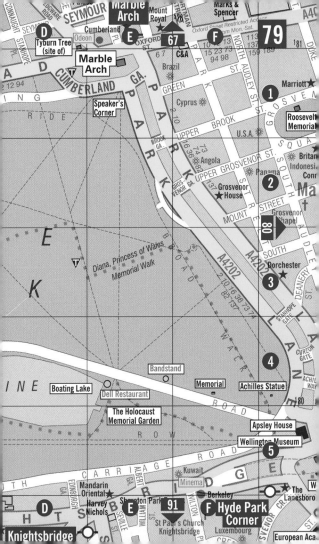

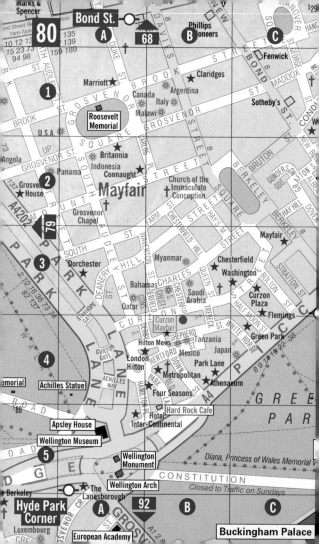

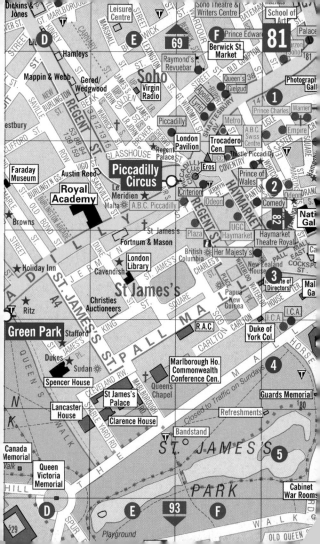

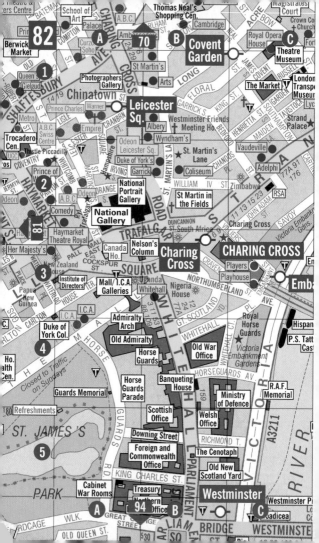

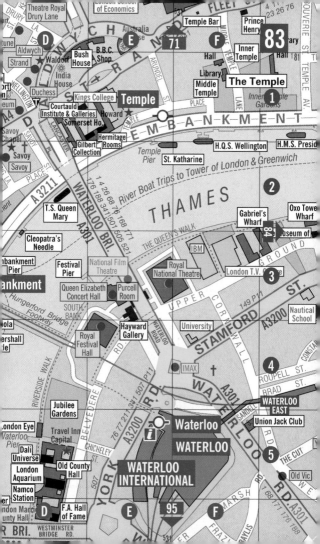

FLEET

e Bar

**Prince's Room**

**84**

Middle **Temple**

Hall

**A**

FRIARS

Crypt Museum

**72**

**B**

NEW PILGRIM ST.

Stationers' Hall

ST. PAUL

CARTER

**C**

Apothecaries' Hall

CARTER

† St. Andrew

College of Arms

QUEEN

Hall

Library

Library

ddle

mple

TUDOR

**The Temple**

**1**

Inner Temple Gardens

Temple

TEMPLE AV.

CARMELITE ST.

BLACKFRIARS UNDERPASS

**Blackfriars**

PUDDLE DOCK

UPPER

WHITE LION HILL

RIVERSIDE

**VICTORIA — EMBKT.**

H.Q.S. Wellington

H.M.S. President

Blackfriars Pier

BLACKFRIARS BRI.

A201

**BLACKFRIARS**

**2**

**R I V E R**

45 63 172

**T H A M E**

**83**

Gabriel's Wharf

The Museum of

Oxo Tower Wharf

London T.V. Centre

**3**

UPPER

CORNWALL

**STAMFORD**

A3200

University

HATFIELD

GROUND

IPC

**ST.**

149 P11

Nautical School

CONSTABLE CRES.

BLACKFRIARS

Bankside Gallery

Express Newspapers

HOPTON ST.

HOLLAND ST.

SUMNE

THE QUEEN'S

ST.

**Tate Mod**

**SOUTHWARK**

149

BURREL ST.

BEAR LANE

Holiday Inn

GAMBIA ST.

SUFFOLK ST.

LAVINGTO

Me

Ban

**Southwark**

**4**

ROUPELL ST.

BRAD ST.

MEYMOTT ST.

**WATERLOO EAST**

loo

RLOO

**WATERLOO**

Union Jack Club

SANDELL ST.

A301

A3200

Young Vic

THE CUT

**Southwark**

A201

Southwark College

UNION

ST.

45 63 172

SURREY ROW

POCOCK

COPPERFI

Knightsbridge

STREE

SUFFOL

**5**

THE ROAD

BLUFFORD

Old Vic

MARSHAL

ROAD

A301

RD.

1 68 171 176 188

**A**

BAYLIS

**96**

**B**

PEPPER RW.

STREET

Teacher

**C**

LANC

532

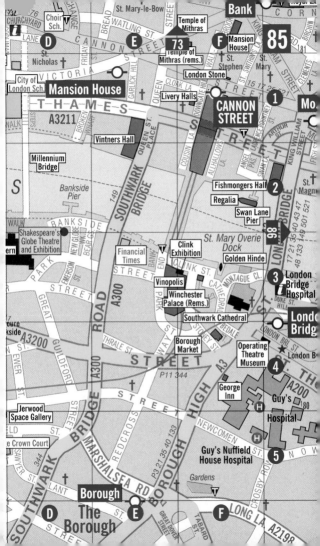

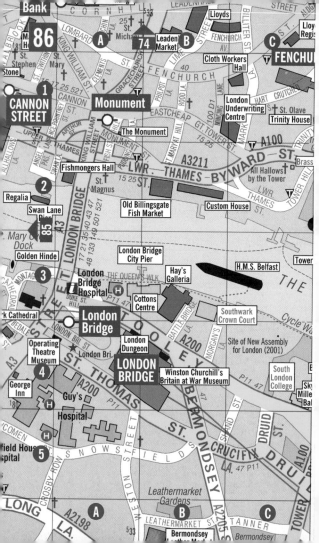

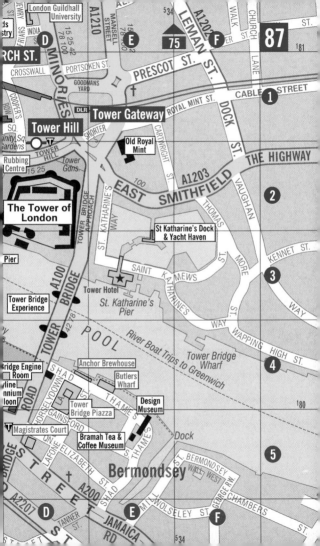

London Guildhall University

A210
MANSELL STREET
INDIA
FRIARS
CROSSWALL
D
E
A1202
LEMAN ST.
F
WALK
CHURCH
LANE
FER
ST.
75
181

PRESCOT ST.

PORTSOKEN ST.
GOODMANS YARD

CABLE STREET ① 

DLR Tower Gateway
Royal Mint St.

**Tower Hill**
SHORTER
CARTWRIGHT ST.
Old Royal Mint
DOCK ST.
THE HIGHWAY

Trinity Sq Gardens
TOWER HILL
Tower Gdns.
EAST SMITHFIELD
100
A1203
VAUGHAN
② 

Rubbing Centre 15 25

**The Tower of London**
TOWER BRIDGE APPROACH
ST. KATHARINE'S WAY
St Katharine's Dock & Yacht Haven
THOMAS ST.
MORE ST.
KENNET ST.
③ 

Pier

A100 TOWER BRIDGE
SAINT KATHARINE'S MEWS
Tower Hotel
St. Katharine's Pier
WAY
WAPPING HIGH ST.
④ 

**Tower Bridge Experience**

POOL
River Boat Trips to Greenwich
Tower Bridge Wharf
180

Bridge Engine Room
Anchor Brewhouse
SHAD
Butlers Wharf
THAMES
Design Museum
Dock
⑤ 

line nnium loon
HORSELYDOWN
GAINSFORD
Tower Bridge Piazza
Bramah Tea & Coffee Museum
BERMONDSEY WALL WEST

Magistrates Court
LAFONE
ELIZABETH
SHAD
ST.
GEORGE R.W.
CHAMBERS

**Bermondsey**

BRIDGE STREET
A2207
D
TANNER ST.
A200
E
MILL
WOLSELEY ST.
F
534
JAMAICA RD.

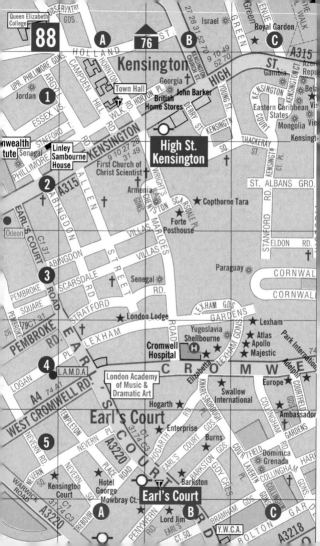

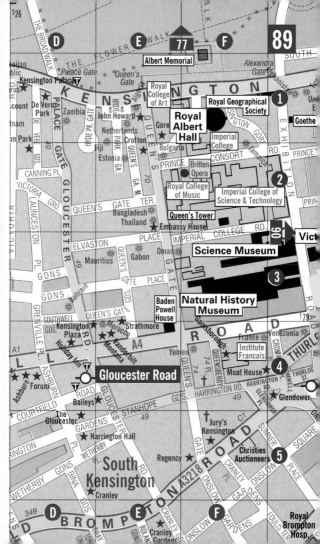

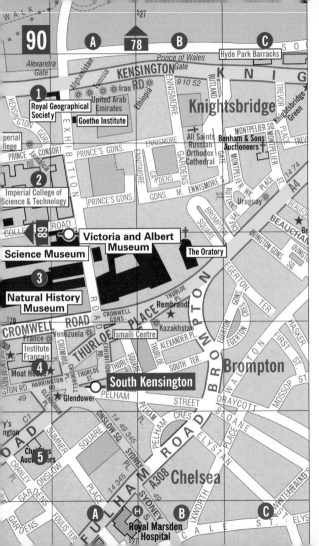

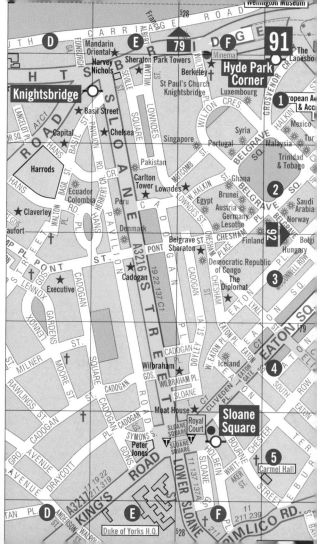

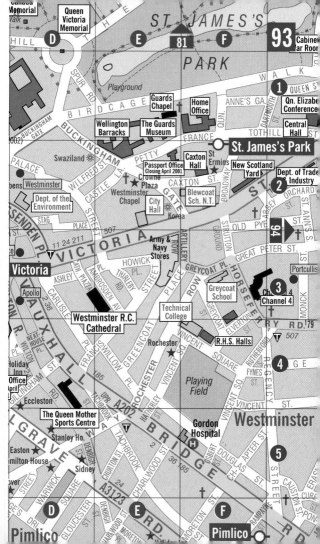

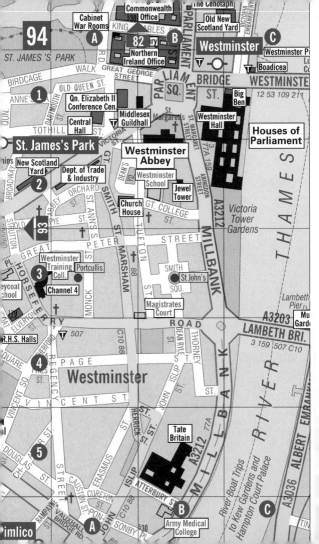

ST. JAMES'S PARK

**A** Cabinet War Rooms

**B** Commonwealth Office · 520 · KING CHARLES · Northern Ireland Office · 82 LY

Old New Scotland Yard

**C** VICTORIA EMBANKMENT

Westminster

Westminster Pi
Lo

Boadicea

The Cenotaph

PARLIAMENT

BRIDGE

WESTMINSTER

WALK

BIRDCAGE

ANNE · ST

OLD QUEEN ST.

DARTMOUTH

WALK

GREAT GEORGE STREET

PAR LIA MENT SQ.

ST.

Big Ben

ST.

12 53 109 211

**1** Qn. Elizabeth II Conference Cen.

Central Hall

TOTHILL ST.

Middlesex Guildhall

St. Margaret's

Westminster Hall

Houses of Parliament

**St. James's Park**

**Westminster Abbey**

VICTORIA

ST.

GT.

BROADWAY

**2** New Scotland Yard

Dept. of Trade & Industry

ABBEY

ORCHARD

PYE

ST.

ST. ANN'S ST.

Westminster School

DEAN'S

YD.

Jewel Tower

ABINGDON STREET

7/7A 159

A3212

Victoria Tower Gardens

THAMES

**93**

Church House

GT. COLLEGE ST.

DEAN

Westminster Training Coll.

SMITH ST.

PETER

ST.

TUFTON

STREET

MARSHAM

SMITH SQU.

MILLBANK

Victoria

Lambeth Pier

**3** Portcullis

Channel 4

88

St John's

HORSEFERRY

Magistrates Court

ROAD

A3203

Mu

LAMBETH BRI.

eycoat school

507

ELVERTON ST.

HERFORD

C10 88

DEAN RYLE

THORNEY

3 159 507 C10

R.H.S. Halls

**4**

PAGE

REGENCY

VINCENT SQ.

ST.

ST.

**Westminster**

VINCENT

ST.

JOHN

HERRICK ST.

RIVER

ALBERT EMBAN

DOUGLAS

**5**

ERASMUS ST.

Tate Britain

A3212

ISLIP

MILLBANK

A3036

CAUSTON SP·ON

CURETON

ATTERBURY

ST.

River Boat Trips

to Kew Gardens and Hampton Court Palace

VAUXHALL BRIDGE RD.

RAMPAYNE

**A** JOHN ISLIP

**B** SONBY PL · 530 · Army Medical College

**C**

imlico

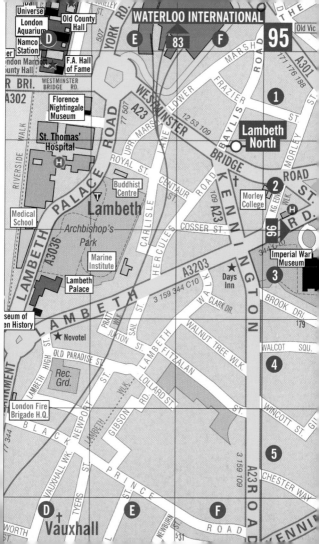

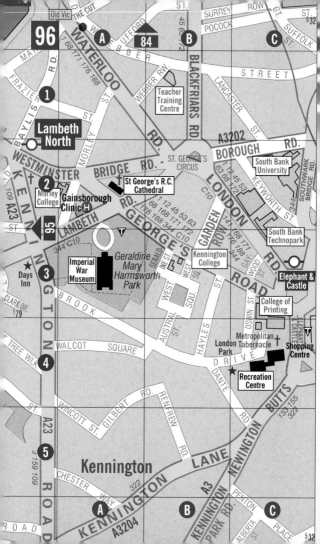

## INDEX TO STREETS

Abbreviations:

All : Alley
App : Approach
Arc : Arcade
Av : Avenue
Bk : Back
Boulevd : Boulevard
Bri : Bridge
B'way : Broadway
Bldgs : Buildings
Bus : Business
Cen : Centre
Chu : Church
Chyd : Churchyard
Circ : Circle
Cir : Circus
Clo : Close
Comn : Common
Cotts : Cottages
Ct : Court
Cres : Crescent
Dri : Drive
E : East
Embkmt : Embankment
Est : Estate
Gdns : Gardens
Ga : Gate
Gt : Great
Grn : Green
Gro : Grove

Ho : House
Ind : Industrial
Junct : Junction
La : Lane
Lit : Little
Lwr : Lower
Mnr : Manor
Mans : Mansions
Mkt : Market
M : Mews
Mt : Mount
N : North
Pal : Palace
Pde : Parade
Pk : Park
Pas : Passage
Pl : Place
Rd : Road
S : South
Sq : Square
Sta : Station
St : Street
Ter : Terrace
Up : Upper
Vs : Villas
Wlk : Walk
W : West
Yd : Yard

101

Grove End Rd. *NW8* —1A 58
(in two parts)
Guilford St. *WC1* —1C 70
Guiltspur St. *EC1* —4C 72

**H**alf Moon St. *W1* —3C 80
Halkin St. *SW1* —1A 92
Hamilton Pl. *W1* —4A 80
Hampstead Rd. *NW1* —2D 61
Hanbury St. *E1* —2E 75
Hanover Ga. *NW1* —4C 58
Hanover Sq. *W1* —5C 68
Hanover St. *W1* —5C 68
Hans Cres. *SW1* —2D 91
Hanson St. *W1* —2D 69
Hans Pl. *SW1* —3E 91
Hans Rd. *SW3* —2D 91
Harcourt St. *W1* —3C 66
Hardwick St. *EC1* —4F 63
Harewood Av. *NW1* —4A 66
Harewood Pl. *W1* —5C 68
Harley St. *W1* —1B 68
Harrington Gdns. *SW7* —5C 88
Harrington Rd. *SW7* —4F 89
Harrington Sq. *NW1* —2D 61
Harrowby St. *W1* —4C 66
Harrow Pl. *E1* —4C 74
Harrow Rd. *W9 & W2* —1A 64
Hart St. *EC3* —1C 86
Hasker St. *SW3* —4C 90
Hastings St. *WC1* —4B 62
Hatfields. *SE1* —3A 84
Hatherley St. *SW1* —5E 93
Hatton Garden. *EC1* —2A 72
Hay Hill. *W1* —2C 80
Hayles St. *SE11* —4B 96
Haymarket. *SW1* —2F 81
Hayne St. *EC1* —2C 72
Hay's M. *W1* —3B 80
Henrietta Pl. *W1* —4B 68
Henrietta St. *WC2* —1C 82
Herbert Cres. *SW1* —2E 91
Herbrand St. *WC1* —5B 62
Hercules Rd. *SE1* —3E 95
Herrick St. *SW1* —5A 94
Hertford Rd. *W2* —4A 64
Hertford St. *W1* —4B 80
High Holborn. *WC1* —4C 70
Highway, The. *E1* —2F 87
Hill St. *W1* —3A 80
Hinde St. *W1* —4A 68
Hobart Pl. *SW1* —2B 92
Hogarth Rd. *SW5* —5B 88
Holbein Pl. *SW1* —5F 91
Holborn. *EC1* —3F 71
Holborn Cir. *EC1* —3A 72
Holborn Viaduct. *EC1* —3B 72
Holland St. *SE1* —3C 84

Holland St. *W8* —1A 88
Holles St. *W1* —4C 68
Holywell La. *EC2* —1C 74
Holywell Row. *EC2* —1B 74
Homer Row. *W1* —3C 66
Hooper St. *E1* —5F 75
Hopton St. *SE1* —3C 84
Hornton St. *W8* —5A 76
Horseferry Rd. *SW1* —3F 93
Horseguards Av. *SW1* —4B 82
Horse Guards Rd. *SW1* —4A 82
Horselydown La. *SE1* —5D 87
Horton Pl. *W8* —1A 88
Houndsditch. *EC3* —4C 74
Howick Pl. *SW1* —3E 93
Howland St. *W1* —2E 69
Hugh St. *SW1* —5C 92
Hunter St. *WC1* —5C 62
Huntley St. *WC1* —1E 69
Hyde Pk. Cres. *W2* —5B 66
Hyde Pk. Gdns. *W2* —1A 78
Hyde Pk. Ga. *SW7* —1E 89
(in two parts)
Hyde Pk. Sq. *W2* —5B 66
Hyde Pk. St. *W2* —5B 66

**I**mperial College Rd. *SW7* —3F 89
India St. *EC3* —5D 75
Inglebert St. *EC1* —3F 63
Inner Circ. *NW1* —4F 59
Inverness Pl. *W2* —1C 76
Inverness Ter. *W2* —5C 64
Ironmonger La. *EC2* —5E 73
Irving St. *WC2* —2A 82
Ivor Pl. *NW1* —1D 67
Ixworth Pl. *SW3* —5B 90

**J**amaica Rd. *SE1* —5E 87
James St. *W1* —5A 68
James St. *WC2* —1C 82
Jermyn St. *SW1* —3D 81
Jewry St. *EC3* —5D 75
Jockey's Fields. *WC1* —2E 71
John Adam St. *WC2* —2C 82
John Islip St. *SW1* —5A 94
John Prince's St. *W1* —4C 68
John St. *WC1* —1E 71
Joiner St. *SE1* —4A 86
Judd St. *WC1* —4B 62
Juxton St. *SE11* —4E 95

**K**emble St. *WC2* —5D 71
Kendal St. *W2* —5C 66
Kennet St. *E1* —3F 87
Kennington La. *SE11* —5A 96
Kennington Pk. Rd. *SE11* —5B 96

Porchester Sq. *W2* —4C 64
Porchester Ter. *W2* —1D 77
Porchester Ter. N. *W2* —4C 64
Portland Pl. *W1* —1B 68
Portman Sq. *W1* —4F 67
Portman St. *W1* —5F 67
Portsoken St. *E1* —1E 87
Portugal St. *WC2* —5E 71
Poultry. *EC2* —5F 73
Praed St. *W2* —4F 65
Pratt Wlk. *SE11* —4E 95
Prescot St. *E1* —1E 87
Primrose St. *EC2* —2B 74
Prince Albert Rd. *NW1 & NW8*
(in two parts) —3B 58
Prince Consort Rd. *SW7* —2E 89
Prince's Gdns. *SW7* —2A 90
(in two parts)
Prince's Sq. *W2* —1B 76
Prince's St. *EC2* —5F 73
Princes St. *W1* —5C 68
Princeton St. *WC1* —2D 71
Procter St. *WC1* —3D 71
Pudding La. *EC3* —2A 86
Puddle Dock. *EC4* —1C 84
Purchese St. *NW1* —2A 62

Quaker St. *E1* —1D 75

Queen Anne's Ga. *SW1* —1F 93
Queen Anne St. *W1* —3B 68
Queen Elizabeth St. *SE1* —5D 87
Queensberry Pl. *SW7* —4F 89
Queensborough Ter. *W2* —1C 76
Queen's Gdns. *W2* —1D 77
Queen's Ga. *SW7* —1E 89
Queen's Ga. Gdns. *SW7* —3E 89
Queen's Ga. M. *SW7* —2E 89
Queen's Ga. Pl. *SW7* —3E 89
Queen's Ga. Ter. *SW7* —2E 89
Queen's Gro. *NW8* —1A 58
Queen Sq. *WC1* —1C 70
Queen St. *EC4* —1E 85
Queen St. *W1* —3B 80
Queen St. Pl. *EC4* —2E 85
Queen's Wlk. *SW1* —4D 81
Queensway. *W2* —4C 70
Queen Victoria St. *EC4* —1B 84

Radnor Pl. *W2* —5B 66

Rampayne St. *SW1* —5F 93
Randolph Av. *W9* —1E 65
Ranelagh Bri. *W2* —3C 64
Rathbone Pl. *W1* —3F 69
Rathbone St. *W1* —3E 69
Rawlings St. *SW3* —5D 91
Ray St. *EC1* —1A 72
Redchurch St. *E2* —1D 75

Redcross Way. *SE1* —5E 85
Redhill St. *NW1* —2C 60
Red Lion Sq. *WC1* —3D 71
Red Lion St. *WC1* —2D 71
Regency St. *SW1* —4F 93
Regent Sq. *WC1* —4C 62
Regent St. *W1 & SW1* —4C 68
Remnant St. *WC2* —4D 71
Renfrew Rd. *SE11* —4B 96
Richmond Ter. *SW1* —5B 82
Riding Ho. St. *W1* —3C 68
Ring, The. *W2* —3B 78
Risinghill St. *N1* —2E 63
Riverside Wlk. *SE1* —2D 95
River St. *EC1* —3F 63
Robert St. *NW1* —4C 60
Rochester Row. *SW1* —4E 93
Rodney St. *N1* —1E 63
Roger St. *WC1* —1E 71
Roland Gdns. *SW7* —5E 89
Rood La. *EC3* —1B 86
Ropemaker St. *EC2* —2F 73
Rosebery Av. *EC1* —1F 71
Rossmore Rd. *NW1* —1C 66
Rotten Row. *SW7 & SW1* —5A 78
Roupell St. *SE1* —4A 84
Royal College St. *NW1* —1F 61
Royal Mint St. *E1* —1F 87
Royal St. *SE1* —2E 95
Rugby St. *WC1* —1D 71
Rupert St. *W1* —1F 81
Russell Sq. *WC1* —2B 70
Russell St. *WC2* —1C 82
Rutherford St. *SW1* —4F 93
Rutland St. *SW7* —2C 90

Sackville St. *W1* —2D 81

Sail St. *SE11* —4E 95
St Albans Gro. *W8* —2C 88
St Andrew St. *EC4* —3A 72
St Ann's St. *SW1* —2A 94
St Ann's Ter. *NW8* —1A 58
St Barnabas St. *SW1* —5A 92
St Botolph St. *EC3* —4D 75
St Bride St. *EC4* —4B 72
St Cross St. *EC1* —2A 72
St Edmund's Ter. *NW8* —1C 58
St George's Cir. *SE1* —2B 96
St George's Dri. *SW1* —5C 92
St George's Rd. *SE1* —2A 96
St George St. *W1* —1C 80
St Giles Cir. *W1* —4A 70
St Giles High St. *WC2* —4A 70
St James's Pl. *SW1* —4D 81
St James's Sq. *SW1* —3E 81
St James's St. *SW1* —3E 81
St John La. *EC1* —2B 72
St John St. *EC1* —1B 72

107

108

## INDEX TO EMBASSIES, LEGATIONS AND COMMONWEALTH REPRESENTATIVES

110

## INDEX TO HOSPITALS